This edition of the

God is responding

is a present to **Sri Balasai Baba** for His 50th birthday on January 14, 2010.

All proceeds from the sale of this book will flow into the charity projects of the divine incarnation, Sri Balasai Baba.

Sri Balasai Baba

God is responding

REVISED 1st EDITION

The photos are property of the
"Sri Balasai-Central-Trust", Kurnool 518001, A.P., India

Layout / cover	Isabell Cathérine Charlé, Germany
Translation / copyright©	Dr. Detlef Angermeier, Germany

Reprints, copies and excerpts of the book produced without authorization are not allowed.
Permission can be obtained in written form from the
"Sri Balasai-Central-Trust", Kurnool 518001, A.P., India

E-Mail	bestellung@sribalasaibaba.at
Publishing house	Association "Helfende Hände" Schulstraße 25 A - 2763 Neusiedl bei Pernitz Austria Phone: + 43 (0) 66 44 50 65 78 www.sribalasaibaba.at
Printing company	Balto Print Utenos g. 41A, Vilnius LT-08217 www.baltoprint.com
ISBN-number	**978-3-940140-15-9**

Acknowledgements

The German version of this book has been compiled by
Mrs. Bernida Zangl and Mrs. G. Gabriel.
The book is based on various interviews with Sri Balasai Baba that took place between 1988 and 2001.

For all their great work and accomplishments we are very grateful.
Many thanks to all the endeavors of the devotees who have worked ceaselessly on the "Balasai Baba News" since 1988.
To all of them we convey deep gratitude for their help and support.

May Sri Balasai Baba bless them all!
We thank profoundly Sri Balasai Baba.

PREFACE

A few years before the birth of Sri Balasai Baba, His parents, on a holy pilgrimage, were told by the famous saint Sri Ramana Maharshi that their son would be born as a divine incarnation.

Sri Balasai Baba grew up in Kurnool, on the premises of the Shirdi Sai temple. His father died when He was still young, so His grandfather and mother took care of Him. Even as a child he already possessed divine powers. He was able to heal the sick simply by touching them. A half-paralyzed person experienced a complete healing simply because Sri Balasai had touched his back.

His first materializations occurred during His childhood. One day He produced hot Indian sweets for His friends. The sweets poured out of His hands and into the outstretched hands of His playmates.

At the age of 18, Sri Balasai Baba founded His first ashram on the premises adjacent to the Shirdi Sai temple. Once the ashram was finished, He constructed His first hospital in which, even today, hundreds of poor and sick people receive medical care.

Sri Balasai Baba is well known all over the world. People from all continents come to see Him, to receive His blessings and to get His advice. Sri Balasai Baba sets an example of living a perfect life in simplicity. He instructs us that we can be successful in our life through selflessness, helpfulness, compassion and the right mental attitude.

Sri Balasai Baba

His message is as follows : Be happy, make others happy and reach me happily.

From Him we learn that we can successfully and harmoniously shape our life by assuming a relaxed inner attitude defined by truth, beauty and love. Sri Balasai Baba is devoid of personal motives and interests. He is devoid of attachments, inclinations and desires. He is always happy. He acts with a power which we call love. An immense, immeasurable and unconditional love. This love represents the true nature of human beings. It is the example that we should all follow.

Sri Balasai Baba neither founded a sect, nor does He represent a particular religious group. People of all classes and faiths come to Him. The symbols of all religions decorate the entrance to His ashram in Kurnool, India.

In India, Sri Balasai Baba is venerated as an avatar *(the embodiment of the divine in a human form)*. Whenever hatred, destruction and violence become too prevalent, an avatar *(such as Rama, Krishna, or Jesus Christ)* appears on earth to show the right way to humans who are willing to listen. God takes the form of a human being *(an avatar)* in order to reconstruct the divine order and to bring back righteousness. This is a service to the world. The avatar comes as a human among humans. He moves among them as a friend and a patron, a relative, a leader, a teacher, a healer and as a participant.

Sri Balasai Baba wants to serve humanity in many ways. He has created an endowment, which supports philanthropic projects in the fields of education and health care. In addition to the free eye surgeries which have been provided by the endowment *(and have had* a 100% success rate), the endowment also runs an extraordinary school in the vicinity of Kurnool. Sri Balasai Residential School is a boarding school for higher learning. The school accommodates about a thousand students, primarily from the federal state of Andhra Pradesh. In only its second year of existence, the school was bestowed with honors by the Indian government. Further projects are currently underway, including a hospital, a hospice and a university.

Apart from the Indian languages such as Telugu, Tamil, Karnataka, Malayalam, Urdu, Hindi and Sanskrit, Sri Balasai Baba also speaks a variety of other languages. Speakers of German, Japanese and English are surprised when Sri Balasai Baba speaks to them in their mother tongue. Through humorous puns, He expresses the jovial easiness of His divine presence.

On January 14, 2004 Sri Balasai Baba was appointed as a chancellor of the University of Raipur, India. On February 26, 2006 He was also appointed Associated President and Chancellor for South India of the International Association of Educators for World Peace (IAEWP), a UN and UNESCO affiliate. In the same year He received two titles of doctor honoris causa one from The Global Peace University of the UNO in Netherlands and the other one from the Université Libre Service des Sciences de l'Homme in Paris, France. In the year 2007 Sri Balasai Baba received the Bachelor of Law from the Bundelkhand University in Jhansi, India. The Open Global University in Amsterdam also appointed Sri Balasai Baba as its extraordinary ambassador and plenipotentiary in July, 2008. In the same year He was conferred the World Theology Award from Global University in Zambia and the World Spirituality Award from the IAEWP.
On August 5/ 2010 Sri Balasai Baba was admitted as an advocate on the Roll of Bar Council of the State of Andrah Pradesh, India.

Sri Balasai Baba

The seeking and questioning human being can, by the grace of God, receive divine responses. This book is based on a series of questions asked by devotees from both the East and the West. In answering, Sri Balasai Baba takes into account not only his own thoughts on the matter at hand, but also the personality and receptiveness of the listener. In his responses one can find a way to live our lives more consciously and to walk the path of divinity.

THE WORDS OF GOD ARE PURE LIGHT.

"Contemplate my messages, for the words of God are simply God Himself. There is no difference!"

"Those who reflect on the words of God, meditate on God."

Sri Balasai Baba

God is responding

Table of Contents

Acknowledgements	09
Preface	11
Advice	21
Anger	24
Animals	26
Aum-OM	27
Ashram	28
Astrology	31
Baba	33
Baba and his devotees	47
Baba's mother	55
Baba's words	60
Bad behavior	61
Bad spirits	65
Bala Tripura Sundari	66
Bhajans - Songs of Praise	67
Blessings	68
Body	69
Books	71
Catastrophes	73
Charity	73
Compassion	75
Concentration	76
Commitment	77
Criticism	78
Darshan	81
Death	82
Detachment	84

Sri Balasai Baba

Devotees 87
Devotion 89
Dharma 91
Difficulties 96
Dreams 98
Earth 99
Effort.. 100
Enlightenment 103
Envy 105
Evil 108
Faith 115
Food 116
Free Will 118
Gifts 119
Goals 119
God 121
Grace 133
Greed 136
Guru-Spiritual Master 136
Happiness 143
Healing 147
Heart 148
Heaven 151
Holidays 152
Indifference 153
Jesus 155
Karma 161
Liberation 173
Life 179
Love 181
Mantra 185
Marriage 187

God is responding

Material Goods	190
Meditation	193
Mind	197
Miracles	199
Money	203
Morality	204
Nature	205
Nightmares	206
Non-Violence	207
Patience	209
Peace	211
Prayer	215
Present	218
Reincarnation	221
Religion	224
Sacrifice	229
Satan	230
Service	232
Sexuality	234
Sin	237
Sleep	238
Social project	239
Spirituality	245
Suffering	247
Suicide	248
Temples	249
Time	250
Wishes	251
Yoga	255
Youth	256
Conclusion	259
Addresses	259

God is responding

A

ADVICE

What follows is the speech that Baba gave to his devotees on New Year's Day, 2001.

BABA: Accept everything that comes from God! **Make no assumptions about the future!** Then there is no happiness or unhappiness, only indifference. Try to be relaxed in all situations. Be happy and content. Do not run after physical and material things; this creates only misfortune. Material happiness is only temporarily. Hidden behind each ephemeral happiness is a subtle sadness.

There is nothing wrong with material happiness, but do not forget divine happiness. Do not forget God's divine bliss. Be happy on all levels, material and spiritual. It does not make sense to suppress worldly desires, since this does not free us or enable us to pursue the spiritual path.

Whatever you do, do it with divine consciousness. To act from divine consciousness means to give everything to God, no matter what it is we do. Even if we commit a sin for which we feel sorry, we lay it at the feet of God. The divine fire burns it and turns it into the good. Love for God and devotion to Him is necessary.

Sri Balasai Baba

Try to learn to discriminate. The swan is the symbol of purity. The swan, by discrimination, swallows only the milk - the good - and leaves the bad, the water. Similarly, you should take the good and leave the bad. **Do not forget to love.** Never give up. You do not need to renounce everything or leave your life behind, just open yourself up to God. Do not be confused, depressed or deceived - be indifferent. **Everything comes from God at the right time.**

Have good relations, but do not get attached. Be free! Be open to God and have the freedom to accept everything that comes. God protects and blesses all His devotees. He takes care of them 24 hours; He protects them. Even during seemingly bad times, when you are sad and you feel depressed, you should be bound to God. True devotees are those who devote themselves to Him. They are protected by Baba on all levels.

Devotee and God are always together. Do not be so egotistical and proud as to try to reach your spiritual goals alone. Be aware that God helps you! Give yourself completely to God. Once you have done this, your ego will disappear and you will be liberated. You will be like God. Why are you selfish? There will be always a person who is wealthier, more beautiful, or more educated than you. We should not be proud of anything. Be emotionally neutral; stay indifferent. Even if we have a fortune, in truth we have received it from others.

Wealth comes and goes. It is like this for all things. We are all instruments of God. Everything comes from God and everything goes back to God. From time to time God gives us exactly what we need, whether it is a piece of furniture or a partner. Good wishes will be fulfilled by God. Most of the time we are unable to differentiate between good and bad wishes.

God is responding

God knows what is best for us. Once God is in our hearts, He will stay there forever, even then if we leave God. Invite God into the temple of your heart and meet Him there with full attention. Do not ruin your life with useless things and do not fill your heart with trash and passion. Bring God into your heart. If you feel yourself hurting, then it is really your ego that is hurt. It is not God's will to hurt you.

The truth cannot be suppressed or hidden. Live in the truth and not in the illusion. The illusory world is useless and impermanent. Your true goal is to return to divine consciousness. For people who are not on the spiritual path, the material world looks like the truth. Come out of the delusion. Do not let your thoughts of joy, sorrow, or revenge overwhelm you.

To the true devotee Baba gives everything. The problem of a true devotee is also the problem of God. It automatically resolves itself in the light of God. God is like our servant; He does everything free of charge. Learn to be friendly, obliging and helpful to others; learn to give and to sacrifice. The divine blessing comes when we make others happy. When you give a rich person 100 rupees, you won't make him happy, for he is already rich. However, the gift of a single rupee to the poor can be an important gift. He will raise both hands and bless you for your compassion. The blessing of someone in need is also a divine blessing.

Sri Balasai Baba

ANGER

Devotee: *Sometimes we are very angry with you, Baba. In such moments we are unable to pray to you. What shall we do then?*

BABA: Be patient. I pray that your anger relents. Suppose you have a little child at home. It jumps around on your lap, pisses in its pants and pulls at your ears and hair. Are you going to beat it? On the contrary! Maybe you want to put a piece of chocolate in its mouth. Such is the relationship between God and His darling, His devotee. You are always my children, no matter what you do.

Imagine how you would treat your beloved pet or your own child. Treat me in the same manner. **I will treat you as you treat me. If you assign me the role of child, I will be your child. If you see me as your father or your husband, then I will be your father or your husband.**

However, you still need to watch how you treat your God, not for my sake, but for the sake of your own karma. Your anger has no effect on me.

Here is a story to illustrate my point: A sinful devotee regularly visited a temple devoted to the God Shiva. He always carried a beating club, wherever he went. At the temple one day, the devotee wanted Shiva to appear and bestow blessings upon Him. When Shiva did not appear, he picked up his club and began beating the statue of Shiva.

Shiva suddenly appeared in front of Him, saying, "What you do is a sin, my child. This is bad karma!" The devotee replied, "I did it! I wanted to make you appear and I have succeeded!" But Shiva reprimanded him: " I did not come to bless you but to tell you that you are accumulating bad karma by your angry behavior! Your action has no real effect on me, but I cannot watch how you will have to suffer for your sins!"

Devotee: *Why do we need to master our words?*

BABA: As the door serves as the entrance to an apartment, so is the mouth the entrance to our body. We eat and speak with the tongue. Sharp, ugly, aggressive and bad words can hurt the feelings of the listener. Friendly, good and encouraging words are life-giving. Therefore, we should not say things that hurt others. We should remember that we will harvest something ugly with ugly words and that with friendly words we can harvest something friendly.

Often it is even better to be silent than to verbalize bad feelings. We should avoid speaking about the personal matters of others, for the words we are inclined to utter could trigger furious feelings towards us.

Sometimes we are inwardly furious and we would like to express this fury. However, it is better to keep the tongue under control and to be silent. It is very important that you control your fury. You should never allow it to control you and to use you as an instrument.

Devotee: *What do you suggest we do when we perceive fury welling up within us?*

BABA: Wherever you are, leave. Go someplace else for a little while. Then the fury will disappear on its own. If you allow anger and fury to take over your life, you will become a criminal.

ANIMALS

Devotee: What shall I do when I see an animal suffering and it cannot help itself?

BABA: If you can help it, then you should. If you cannot help, then you should close your eyes and ask God to intervene. That is enough. You cannot save every animal. You might help one animal, but how many animals are in the world who suffer? Concentrate on yourself first. Then you will be able to do good things on your path.

Devotee: Nowadays many people sacrifice their lives to save animals. Is that a waste?

BABA: No, they are certainly doing something good. God is present whenever good things are done. If you do something good and you think about me, then it will be very good. I will be very happy. With good actions we can neutralize bad karma. If you do good things now, then your next life will be easy. Your actions should benefit others.

I love dogs very much, because they are the only creatures that have the ability to bind themselves to a master. They have a divine imprinting in their brains that makes this possible. You can beat a dog, or yell at it, but it will always return to you again. A dog is capable of feeling emotion, just like a human. But it cannot express its feelings as a human would. So it transmits its feelings in its own manner. Look how it loves you - indescribable.

All beings in the world have feelings, even the trees and the plants. If you take the time to observe, you can learn a lot from nature. God lives in all parts of creation. If you harm a living being, that is an act against God.

AUM-OM

Devotee: *What is the meaning of the word 'Aum'?*

BABA: Before the beginning of the universe, the formless God created the sound Aum. Every being derived its existence from this original sound. All creation is pervaded by Aum. Aum is everywhere. Even the sound of the air conditioning in this room contains the vibration of Aum. Aum consists of sound and stillness. Everywhere in nature, if you listen carefully you can find this duality of sound and stillness.

Aum consists of three letters: A, U and M. If you sing the sound of Aum, you should not sing each letter individually. The sounds need to merge with each other. The sound A stems from the navel area, but merges right away into the U. The sound rises within you and ends between your eyebrows or on the highest part of your head, where the M blends into the stillness.

ASHRAM

(Note: An ashram is a sacred meeting place where spiritual aspirants come to pray, worship, meditate and study under the direction of a guru, saint, holy person, or divine incarnation.)

Devotee: *What is an ashram?*

BABA: An ashram is a holy place. It is consecrated either to a saint or to a saint and his devotees. The inhabitants of an ashram usually live only for God and desire to be one with Him.

An ashram can, however, be like a jungle, where many different kinds of animals dwell. A lot of different characters come here. Some lie, some betray. Some try to pull you away from the path. Be aware of that; do not step into the trap. Only participate in conversations with God and do not go astray. Tell yourself: **I came only here because of Baba. I am not interested in anything else. I concentrate on Baba and follow all his words.**

Devotee: *What is this ashram called?*

BABA: Sri Nilayam – the dwelling of the goddess Sri.

Devotee: *Is it a peaceful place?*

BABA: Peace is only one aspect of God. Here you find everything: Love, peace, health, welfare and happiness. It is a pure, holy and auspicious place.

Devotee: *Of what, in particular, should I be aware during my stay in this* *ashram?*

BABA: **Nowhere else will you find this love and proximity to God. Here at the ashram, we learn through practice.** Theory and practical life should go hand in hand, otherwise all the knowledge stays only in the head, where it cannot do anything useful. In India there are numerous saints who teach from the Holy Scriptures, but whose way of living does not match their teachings. **Here we emphasize that the theory needs to be put into practice.**

People come from far away and sacrifice much to come to an ashram. It is difficult and expensive to come. And what do they do when they get here? They go into the city, make idle chat for hours, sleep for half a day and in between they eat. For these things you might as well stay at home. When you come to an ashram, you should orient yourself along spiritual dimensions.

Take the opportunity to meditate, pray, sing holy mantras and concentrate absolutely on God. Do not be satisfied to sing songs of praise for only a few hours a day.

Devotee: How come some people come to you only six or eight times and then never again? Is this the will of God?

BABA: Everybody comes to me because of some relationship in a past life. **You will come as often as your karmic history allows.** If somebody is happy with his time at the ashram, he will never need to come again. If you desire more progress and you decide to continue, then by grace of Baba, the spiritual relationship will continue and you will advance on the spiritual path.

Devotee: What are the rules in an ashram?

Sri Balasai Baba

BABA: You come here to be in the holy presence of Baba, to meditate and to concentrate completely upon the Lord. **Do not be distracted by outside conditions or circumstances. Always focus upon me and ignore everything else.** You are not here to observe others, to judge or to criticize. You are here for yourself. You are here because of your own spiritual development and your spiritual relationship with me. Always be aware of that!
I move directly among you. I play with you. I eat with you. I give you spiritual instructions, when the time is right. Do not forget who I am. I behave as your friend, but you should not violate the borders of respect for your divine teacher.

Devotee: Here are some general rules established by the ashram management:

1. Only approach Baba when he calls you.

2. When you sit together with Baba, do not approach Him without his consent.

3. Only ask Baba questions when He grants you permission to do so.

4. Come to each meeting with Baba having taken a shower and with fresh clothing on.

5. Your clothing should reach your ankles if you do not wear traditional Indian clothes.

6. Smoking, alcohol, drugs and the consumption of meat in the ashram are all strictly forbidden.

7. After the evening singing of songs, you may not leave the ashram.

This is for your own security as well as the security of the ashram.

8. Also for the sake of security, do not create friendships with the Indian people. You should not exchange any addresses or phone numbers with Indians.

9. To give money to beggars supports their bad habits; therefore Baba tells us to refrain from that.

10. In the ashram you should take your laundry down from the ropes by 18:00 hrs.

11. You must participate in the singing of bhajans (songs of praise) every morning and every evening.

Devotee: *Is it useful to wear white clothing?*

BABA: Dress in white clothes. White is a very good color, since it symbolizes the divine light. It is a holy color. It represents purity and peace. Additionally, if you wear white, everybody can see right away that you belong to the ashram and to Baba. In this way you will always be remembered as someone who lived a holy life, only for God.

ASTROLOGY

Devotee: What do you think about astrology?

BABA: Once upon a time a young man went to an astrologer. He wanted to know his future. The astrologer told him that he would get a new vehicle very soon. The man was overwhelmingly happy about this. He cheered and joyfully went home. Full of high spirits, he did not see a trench on his right side of the road. He had an accident and was badly hurt. At the hospital, he was told that he would not be able to walk anymore and that he would need to sit in a wheelchair.

So what kind of new vehicle was he promised? We should carefully consider the meaning of the messages we receive. What is most important is that which God tells us.

Let's say you go to an astrologer and you pay him five hundred euro to tell you about your future. He tells you that a mountain will fall upon you and bury you. Will this be useful information for you? The astrologer cannot protect you, but God can! Therefore it is better to give 500 euro to God and to ask for His protection. Only God has the power to prevent the mountain from falling upon you.

B

BABA

Devotee: *Baba, who are you?*

BABA: I am God in a human form. I am the cause of creation, preservation and destruction. The entire universe is the stage of the Lord. There He plays His divine games: Creation, preservation and dissolution of all things relative and ephemeral.

I am the incarnation of the divine mother, Bala Tripura Sundari, the divine force of creation. This is the first time I have has taken a male form. In former times she always came to earth in a female form.

God incarnates by the virtue of divine will. The humans, who have called Him, need help. Sometimes the help is best given by a male force. Sometimes it is best given by a female force. If the mother is needed, then an incarnation of the elemental force Shakti comes to teach us love and affection. Baba is this Goddess in male form.

I am everything and at the same time I am nothing. I am your mirror. If you stand in front of the mirror, whose face do you see? - Your own. You only laugh. Whose face laughs in the mirror? Only your own. Here it is the same: If you look at me, then I look at you. If you love me, then I love you. I am nothing other than love!

Sri Balasai Baba

Baba possesses a form, but at the same time he is formless. Baba is without characteristics. At the same time he possesses all characteristics. He is everything. Shiva is the only God within the trinity of Brahma, Vishnu and Shiva who is venerated both in his worldly form and in his formless state. Statues of Brahma and Vishnu are venerated, but Shiva is venerated both as a statue and as a formless being.

For me there is neither male nor female. In reality I am the highest light - and the light is genderless. I am everything in one.

Devotee: *Could you please help me to comprehend this better?*

BABA: A formless light has taken a form to live as a human being, in a human body, within human society. My purpose is to teach humans to love and to practice kindness. I guide them on the right way, the spiritual way. Later I bestow unto them liberation, wisdom and enlightenment. I live among you so that everyone will unite as one family.

To a normal person, God looks like a normal human being. Only his devotees will recognize Him as God. If a blind person looks into the mirror, he cannot recognize his own beauty. Only those who have light in their eyes can see themselves in the mirror. Only those who have love, devotion and confidence can experience me in my true form.

I am everything and at the same time I am nothing. I am your mirror. If you stand in front of the mirror, whose face do you see? Your own. Now you are laughing. Whose face laughs in the mirror? Always your own. Here it is the same. As you look at me, so shall I look at you. As you love me, then shall I love you. I am nothing other than your own mirror.

The divine mother, Bala Tripura Sundari, came to my mother in a dream. Bala Tripura Sundari is an embodiment of Shakti, the creative life-giving force of the universe. She told my mother that she *(my mother)* would give birth to an incarnation of Bala Tripura Sundari. Sundari rules over the three Gods – Brahma, Vishnu and Shiva, as well as their partners and worlds. In Sanskrit, Bala means 'Eternal, youthful, beautiful and powerful girl'. She is the life-giving power without which no existence is possible.

It is the first time that the divine mother, Bala Tripura Sundari, (Shakti) has taken a male form. Hence the name, Balasai Baba.

I am the embodiment of pure Shakti (the creative power of the universe). I am the highest divine principle. Everything originates from me. All creation came out of me. Even Brahma, Vishnu and Shiva have their origin in me. Shakti is a formless energy; it is normally manifested in the form of a female avatar. However, in this incarnation it has taken a male body because in India especially it would be difficult for men to accept a female avatar. **Do not have any expectations or ideas about how I have to appear or what I have to do!**

The shakti that I embody is the power in the universe that supplies all living creatures with life energy. It is the invisible power that animates and moves all things. It is the power that makes you see and hear. Shakti is like a big power station that supplies all the houses on earth. For your mortal eyes it is as invisible as the current that flows through electrical wires.

Shakti is like a gold nugget from which the goldsmith can shape any number of gold jewelries. Gold stays gold. This shakti is neither female, nor male, nor neutral. God is female, male and neutral, all at

Sri Balasai Baba

once. He is without any characteristics, like a mirror that reflects everything projected upon it. If you want to see God in a physical form, he looks like Rama, Krishna, Jesus, Buddha. He assumes the form by which you call Him. **God is formless and nameless.**

Because of their earthly desires, human beings are locked into a cycle by which they will come into the world, die and be reborn. God manifests Himself as a human being in order to help human beings overcome the cycle of suffering.

Devotee: *How can this mighty Shakti power assume the little form of Balasai Baba?*

BABA: A small fire can set ablaze the entire universe. Are you not happy to see me in this small form?

Devotee: *Baba, please tell us more about your life.*

BABA: One day, when I was still a little baby and my parents had not yet given me a name, my mother was busy cooking. I was lying in another corner of the room. All of a sudden, a cat started strolling around her, crying ceaselessly. She wondered how the cat had appeared from nowhere. She suddenly felt something terrifying and ran immediately to the corner where I was sitting.

A big king cobra had wrapped itself around me. Her front body was erected and her head was held as if she were guarding me. My mother was profoundly frightened. She believed, out of ignorance, that the snake threatened me. Out of fear that I might be bitten, she sacrificed all her incense sticks, which she lit and put on the floor in front of her. She prayed deeply that the snake go away. Shortly thereafter the snake disappeared.

God is responding

After this incident, my mother brought me to a priest to give me a name. When she told him about the visit of the snake, the priest proposed the name Sesha *(Sesha means snake and Sai means divine mother)*. My grandfather, who lived with us, always called me "Sai Baba" because he had difficulty pronouncing "Sesha Sai" and because our house was adjacent to the Shirdi Sai temple. The inner court of this temple was my favorite place. There I played and spent most of my time. My grandfather brought me to school as well. When my teacher asked him about my name, he responded: "His name is Sai Baba."

Devotee: *Baba, as a child, did you already possess miraculous forces?*

BABA: Yes, but I did not know about them. As a small boy, I used to run down to the river to swim. One day I saw how a woman helped a one-sided paralyzed man cross the river. He was holding himself up on a stick to reach a sandy spot at the bank of the river. With her help, he sat down at the river. She put a towel around her shoulder and went to another spot to bathe.

While trying to wash himself, a gust of wind blew away the man's towel. With all his might he reached out for the towel without any success. I observed this incident from some distance and ran to catch his towel, for I felt compassion for him. With joy he took the towel. While I was standing with him I softly touched his paralyzed shoulder. Not knowing what had happened, I said farewell to him and ran back to the temple.

He felt some change in his body and noticed that his paralysis had completely disappeared. Suddenly he could move freely again. His wife came back and discovered what had happened. He himself could not believe that he was healed through a miracle. "What was the name of

Sri Balasai Baba

this boy?" she wanted to know. But her husband had not asked for my name. He simply remembered that the boy was very beautiful and had an unusual crown of curly hair. Immediately she knelt down at the embankment of the river and thanked God from the depth of her heart.

She did not want to return home without thanking Shirdi Sai Baba for his grace. So they came up to the temple. The man recognized me immediately because of my hair. He rushed to me, knelt down and bowed at my feet, full of gratitude and joy. The woman asked me: "What is your name, Babu *(little boy)*?" My name is Sai Baba," I replied.

Devotee: Baba, what is your life like?

BABA: My life is very boring. Nothing exciting happens, nothing bad and nothing good. Sometimes I create my own problems in order to solve them. They do not concern mundane or personal things; once I have solved a problem, the entire universe moves one step forward. Only God behaves in this way. Humans try to avoid problems, for they only want physical well-being. God is the creator of all problems; for Him it is a pleasure to solve them. Because you identify yourself with your body, you think that your problems belong to you. **But you are not this body. You are eternal, imperishable. You are God, You are His creation.**

Devotee: Your eyes are always everywhere, Baba?

BABA: I do not only see with my physical eyes. I can see everything, everywhere, at any time. I am a guardian. The guardian that always protects is the Lord. **God always protects and guards His adherents. Be aware that each moment God is within you. Then it is impossible that you think, say, or do anything wrong.**

God is responding

Devotee: *You always listen very patiently...*

BABA: This is my nature. Regardless of what happens to me, I will always listen patiently, laughingly, carefully, lovingly and happily. Once, on my birthday, I laid here on my sofa. My body was on a big cushion and my feet were stretched out. While I was talking to one of my devotees, another man came and bit my foot. Yes, he bit into my big toe until blood came out. The man wanted to test me. Laughing, I asked one of my security guards to take the man away. He had already repented his deed and asked me for forgiveness. A lot of people come to test me and to see miracles. Miracles are very popular nowadays. **But God is the greatest of all miracles.**

Devotee: *If you are God, can you learn anything? Can you perform anything with the power of divine will?*

BABA: Yes, yes, but this is very boring. Of course I can do anything within one second. I can count all the grains of sand on the earth within one second. And then? What happens next? This is why I behave like a normal human being!

Devotee: *I would like to see your astral body.*

BABA: Mahatmas, holy people and yogis devote themselves to me, one birth after another. They are ready to accept any pains or difficulties in order to see me in a physical form. And you want to see my astral body? You cannot see it! It is like darkness and light. You cannot see the darkness. If you are not able to examine me in this physical form, how will you then be able to see my astral body? First try one thing. The other thing will come to you automatically. Right now you are not able to pay attention to me for two seconds without thinking about the external world. If you really want to become one with God, you have to dedicate yourself to God, all the time, 24 hours a day. Your interest for society and for yourself must vanish. Only He matters. But reaching this stage requires many reincarnations. If you concentrate on my form and truly make an effort to keep it alive in yourself, you will get what you seek without even asking. If your desires are honest, then I will give you everything.

One day, a man asked me how he could become one with God. I gave him this advice: dedicate your life to service. Work for human beings and you will find God in your work. You do not need to do any spiritual exercises; you do not even need to come for my blessing. Everything you do in the service of others will come back to you.

But he did not follow my words. **You have to follow my words.** Instead he asked me again, "How can I reach God?" You have already reached Him; you are close to me. However, you should never believe that you have reached Baba truly. On the contrary, you should keep reciting His name and seeing his form. You have to keep yearning for Him. Only then you will be united with me beyond this life.

I do not know feelings like joy or affliction. Eating and the like are not important to me. I do not think at all. What I tell you comes directly out of my mind. Now I talk to you, but when you are gone, I will forget everything immediately.

Devotee: *Do you know joy and suffering?*
BABA: The words joy and suffering I do not know. They are not a part of my vocabulary. They belong to the vocabulary of an unenlightened human being who has desires and needs. **If we live each moment consciously and accept everything that comes in a relaxed manner, we can always be in bliss.** Enlightenment is like the morning

after a nightmare, when you wake up and notice with relief that you have only been dreaming.

Devotee: Do you know sorrows?

BABA: Sometimes my heart is a little bit heavy with the sorrows of my devotees and the entire world. But from my mother I learned to accept everything and smile. Why should I burden others with my sorrows? That's why I keep silent about the serious problems that exist. *(Baba inhales and exhales once deeply)*. Look - that's how I do it. Whenever you worry, inhale deeply and expel the burdens with your breath. Even when my mother laid dead in front of me, I did not weep with eyes full of tears. I felt the pain as a weight on my chest. My face felt heavy. First I swallowed, then I inhaled and exhaled profoundly. Then I smiled to console the bereaved.

Devotee: *You do not have any thoughts or feelings, but you still suffer for humanity? How is that possible?*

BABA: My heart has already died an infinite number of deaths for you human beings. I can easily stand it if somebody insults me, cheats me, or tries to hurt me. But I cannot stand it if one of my devotees has to suffer.

Devotee: It is difficult for me to remember at the same time your name and your form.
BABA: Because you still lack love.

Devotee: How can I develop this love?
BABA: **By thinking about me. Think about who I am, what I do and how it is when you are with me. Singing bhajans *(songs of***

praise) also helps. Additionally, to think about Baba, to eat for Baba, to travel for Baba, to work for Baba, to live for Baba – all that is meditation. Do everything with the right attitude. Do it for Baba and because of Baba.

Devotee: Why are you here in a human form?

BABA: Nowadays the dharma *(righteous actions)* have been lost. When humans fail to love each other, God reincarnates to re-establish the dharma and make sure that humans love and respect each other. He takes a human form to make them all happy and to convey to them how precious human life is. It is the wish of God that humans live peacefully and happily.

Devotee: Have you been on earth in a human form before?

BABA: **Yes, God takes always a form when the time and the circumstances demand it.** God lives among human beings. He behaves like an innocent child, like a normal woman, like a normal man. That's why we do not recognize Him. If you recognize His divinity, you will feel His greatness and be happy.

Devotee: How can we reach the transcendent God beyond your form?

BABA: Why do you want that? That is not necessary! **Love of God can only be developed through a divine form.** At the right time you will melt with God and experience the blessings and grace of God.

Devotee: You say that you are God on earth. Are you the only one who is currently here?

BABA: **For human beings there might be a lot of incarnations of God on earth, but if you ask me then the answer is as follows:**

God is responding

I am the one God. I am in each of you and every one of you is in me. Should the humans believe that there are other incarnations on earth, then each incarnation is a part of me and I am also part of each incarnation.

Devotee: Have you conveyed messages to a human in the form of a bird?

BABA With my willpower I can convey messages as a bird, as a lion, as an elephant or as an ant. **For God no form is impossible. Even without a form He can convey messages. Even without any form, God can talk to humans via their own inner voice.** God can assume any form. You cannot guess in advance how He will chose to meet you.

Devotee: What do you have in common with Christ?

BABA: In biblical times, Jesus Christ told the people that they should love each other. Here and now I tell the people that they should love each other and live in peace with each other; they should create peace, happiness and joy. Love each other and try to be loved by others.

Devotee: Baba, did we come to you by chance or are we here because you have called us?

BABA: You have been in a karmic cycle for many lives. Our being together now is not by chance; it is intended.

Devotee: Where do I find you?

BABA: **Wherever we are on this earth, we should be able to sit down and go inside and simply be happy. Dependence on form creates unnecessary suffering. We go inside, talk to God and He listens. It is very easy!**

Sri Balasai Baba

Devotee: *On our way to becoming one with you, do we need to reach a state at which we don't have to concentrate on form any more?*

BABA: No, it is not like that. Be happy when you are with me and be happy when you are not with me. Once you have discovered me within yourself, there won't be any sadness anymore.

When a delicious meal is prepared and waits in front of you, do you eat it, or do you only imagine eating it? When you want to eat, then eat. And when there is a form of God, then concentrate on that. The joy is greater than focusing on the formless.

Devotee: *We need your outer form to find you in ourselves?*

BABA: Yes, to develop love and respect. You should treat my outer form with love and respect. Then you will see God in yourself and treat Him the same way. **You have to learn to be gentle and friendly with the God within. Your internal and external behavior must be identical.** First learn to behave well outwardly.

Devotee: *When did you become aware that you are a divine incarnation?*

BABA: When I was a young boy, my mother repeatedly asked me what I would become later in life. My response was always the same. I wanted to dedicate myself to human beings. When we sacrifice our house for other people, then all houses of the world belong to us. When we sacrifice our lives for God, then we will belong to Him.

Here on earth, everything runs according to certain laws. It is like young boys and girls: until a certain age, there is no difference between their bodies, but all of a sudden their sex develops without any outside influence. It simply happens. At a certain age, my divinity simply manifested.

Devotee: My heart becomes very heavy whenever I leave you.

BABA: Who goes away from whom? You have given me your heart; therefore I live in your heart. There is no separation. A soon as you think of me, I am connected with you. Remember me always!

Devotee: If I have a problem, then I will think of you and it will disappear?

BABA: **Thinking of me is like meditation. Repeating my name is like calling me on the phone. Constantly repeating my name is like wearing a bullet-proof vest.**

Devotee: Baba, please help us to recognize that you are both in us and also everywhere else. How can we do that?

BABA: This requires consciousness. Human beings do not know anything about God. That is why they think He is far away from them. If they knew how close He is to them, they would not hurt Him. **You do not know anything about God, but He knows everything about you.** If you have a child, you know that you are responsible for it, no matter what. You are its mother or father. It is your child. It is the same with God. You are His children, no matter what.

Devotee: What is the difference between Sai and Baba?

BABA: What is the difference between mother and father? Do you want to know why I have chosen this name? So that you can call me whenever you need me. That is why I have taken a name. That is all.

Devotee: Baba, I want to be sure that I will never forget you. Please help me.

Sri Balasai Baba

BABA: It is you who needs to take action. Tell yourself that from today on, you will only live and die for Baba. If it will be helpful for you, take a sheet of paper and write on it: I live and die for Baba. Put this sheet somewhere where you will see it often. In your daily meditation you can pray, "Baba, please give me the power to remember you always."

Devotee: *I am sad when you do not appear to give your blessings.*

BABA: You should never be sad when I do not appear. God does not meditate because He does not need to. If on some occasion I do not come, do not worry about it. Do not ask anybody for me. An avatar *(divine incarnation)* is not a person who has acquired supernatural powers. The avatar comes to earth with spiritual powers. For Him no meditation or recitation of names is necessary.

Devotee: *There are people who claim that Baba speaks through them.*

BABA: **You should not say that Balasai Baba speaks through you. You should not speak in the name of Baba.** This avatar *(divine incarnation)* is among you; you have the great luck to be able to address Him directly. If it is beneficial to share your inner experiences with others, then you can do so.

Devotee: *During the holy fire ceremony, you appear completely different than you normally do.*

BABA: In the future you will experience me differently yet. I am never the same. In the morning, in the afternoon, in the evening - I am always different. Sometimes I am a male, sometimes I am a female. I am the highest power.

Devotee: And how can we recognize Thy greatness?

BABA: You are unable to recognize my divinity. God has degraded Himself to be your servant. God is the servant of the servants.

Devotee: Do you also work at night?

BABA: For me the night is the day and the day is the night.

BABA AND HIS DEVOTEES

Devotee: And what about my life?

BABA: If you have put your life into my hands, then I will take full responsibility for it! Do your best at each moment; leave the consequences to me. Whether they are good or bad, they will be my responsibility.

To think about Baba is more effective than any remedy. Nothing can happen to you if you think of me. I am always with you. **Before you go anywhere, I will cover you with a protective shield.** Nobody goes away from here with empty hands. I let everyone depart happily and I give him what he needs, whether he asks for it or not. I am a ferryman, bringing the waiting passengers in his boat safely from one bank to the other. If they want to cross the river, they need to get into my boat. Only then can I take them across.

Some sit in front of God and think that they are bigger than Him. It is like a monkey turning somersaults in front of a mountain. Those who go to a spiritual master should forget all they know and be ready to

Sri Balasai Baba

learn new things. God is like an ocean. No matter how much water you scoop from the ocean, you cannot empty it. **Even a good devotee will never have the feeling that he truly knows God in all His profundity.**

I ask you to remember the words you hear here and to put them into practice. I do not want to see you encounter difficulties. You come here from distant countries. Sometimes I am very sad that you sacrifice much to come here, but then you do not put my teachings into practice.

Devotee: *Often, when I sit in the garden, I expect that you might come to me.*

BABA: Some people expect me to appear in their rooms. Others expect me to appear in some corner of the building. Others sit in different parts of the ashram and expect me there. Because I am always bowing to my devotees, my shoulder has begun to give me pain. And still it is not enough for most people. **From the physical point of view, I cannot fulfill all expectations. But mentally I am constantly with each of you. Our relationship is a mental one, not a physical one. The relationship between God and the devotee is a relationship from heart to heart and from soul to soul.**

Whatever you do - whether you are walking, standing, relaxing, or working, connect your heart to my heart. In this manner, you will experience that I am always with you. **Since I live in the heart of my devotee, I am always with my devotee. The heart of my devotee is my temple and my residence.**

Devotee *(Baba had been coughing for a few days): Can we make Baba sick?*

BABA: If the devotees dedicate themselves completely to God, then their problems and diseases pass automatically to the divine incarnation. Even if the devotees have not asked me to take on their problems and diseases, the diseases still come to me. It is like a magnet. Whether the magnet wants it or not, all nearby iron will be attracted to it and stick to it. **God is like a huge fireball. Whatever falls into it will be burnt.** Whatever you offer God is for your own benefit, not His.

Devotee: Baba, why do divine beings often suffer so immensely?

BABA: That happens to set an example. It discloses the greatness of a soul, which is necessary to attract God. Only through the body of such a great soul is it possible that God can be born on earth.

Devotee: When I have spiritual questions, can I talk to you about them privately?

BABA: Only during a private conversation will I discuss the spiritual practices you need to advance on your path. **If I talk to you alone, then you need to be very alert.** In general you should listen carefully whenever I speak. In a personal interview, you need to pay attention to symbolic meaning. **Do not pay any attention to the spiritual experiences of others. Each man has his own spiritual experiences according to his disposition.** You will have your own divine experiences.

Devotee: Do we need to travel to India to progress spiritually?

BABA: No, of course not. You can think about me at home! If you want to come here, you need to have a passport, to book a flight and so on. I do not need all this! Call me and I will come to you. You do not need a telephone to call me. **Pray to me - that is sufficient**.

Devotee: *Sometimes I feel your presence in my room. I ask myself: is this real or is this my imagination?*

BABA: The moment that you think and feel that I am present, I am present. It is certainly not imagination.

Devotee: *I can only think of you as long as I am awake. Once I fall asleep I do not know what happens.*

BABA: As long as you are aware of yourself, you should think about me. Once you fall asleep, I come and take care of you. Throughout life, we should think about God. Then He will come at the moment of our death and He will be very near to us.

Devotee: *Baba, do you already know everything I am going to ask you?*

BABA: I always behave like an innocent child: deliberately uniformed. Only in this way can a conversation take place between us. How else could we communicate with each other? Before you start to talk, I already know what you want to say. I have no degree in English and no speaking practice, but I still speak to you in English, even using difficult words.

Devotee: *Baba, should I transfer everything to you and then you will do everything?*

BABA: Some people say to Baba: "Oh Baba, in myself there is evil, negativity, envy, jealousy and anger. But everything is from you, so you have to take it away." I cannot do something like that. I cannot take those things away. There are some among my devotees who do not make any efforts to change. They simply say, "Baba, do this for me!" **You**

God is responding

have to do everything yourself.

If you put in all your efforts, then God's grace will help you **to eliminate all the negative characteristics with which you were born. But if you cannot even control your mind, how can I help you?** Whenever negative thoughts emerge, replace them with positive thoughts. You can hypnotize yourself by sending out positive thoughts and commands.

Devotee: Can I always be close to you?

BABA: You cannot always be close to me. Sometimes I generate an artificial distance to test you. Then you have the feeling that you are very far from me. **But you have to continue your path. Do not ever leave it!**

Devotee: Baba, you say that we need to find you in our hearts; you say that we have to aspire for eternal bliss. On the other hand, you tell us that many saints and the yogis devote their lives to seeing Baba. Why should we look for you in our hearts only? If we do not see you for three days, we suffer terribly.

BABA: No, you should not do that! You should be happy when you see me and when you do not see me. Try to keep the feeling of contentment and happiness in your heart. Wherever I am, be happy, for I am always with you. **Pray that you may get the opportunity to see me again tomorrow. Your hearts need to yearn for me, so that I will come to you.**

Devotee: If God is everywhere, why is it necessary to come here at all? What difference does is make to be here with the form of God?

BABA: Some are only content if they see the divine form. It can be a

Sri Balasai Baba

special grace, because:

1. To look at God in the eyes can make one aware of the sins one has committed.
2. To hear God's voice burns sins that were committed by the ears.
3. To touch God's feet burns all sins that were committed with the body.

Devotee: *Baba, you said that the morning sun is not that good for us?*

BABA: This is only relevant for those who lay down in the sun to get a nice tan. Or for those who sit down at a nice sunny place instead of working. You should never say that Baba said this or that without contextualizing my statement. A single attorney works on many cases. Each case requires different arguments in order to be successful. Here it is the same. To one person I might say this or that is good for him. To another person I might say exactly the opposite. Everyone's case is different.

Devotee: *Baba, I once saw a white-yellow light around your head. It transferred to other people. What was it?*

BABA: What you see is spiritual power. My true essence is pure light, but in this world I have taken a form. You are a fortunate child, for only one among thousands of people look beyond form to the realm of light.

Devotee: *Baba, I saw in someone else's aura that same light!*

BABA: This is the reflection of her divine experiences. A person who is completely directed towards God reflects the divine light. A devotee who is totally dedicated to Baba reflects His divine light.

God is responding

Devotee: *Baba, how long have we known each other?*

BABA: It may seem that everything happens by chance, **but there are no coincidences.** Not by chance are you now with me. In past lives we knew each other, but you were unable to recognize who I really was. So now we meet once again. According to the karmic law, you harvest now what you have sown in your past life. It may be that you will be bound to me for a while and then lose contact again.

Karma makes you come and go. You do not remember who you were in your former life and how you have developed personally. You may be in another body, but the Atman - the soul - remains the same. Our body is perishable, but our soul is not. Even I have a different form; this is one of the reasons why you cannot recognize me. You do not know who I am, but you are drawn back to me, because you want to find out everything about God. This is precisely your duty. One day your soul will merge with me. But as long as you are ignorant, you should trust and believe me. The problem is: I know that you are my children, but you do not know that I am your father.

Devotee*: What sort of relationship existed between you and me in former lives?*

BABA: It does not matter. It is not verifiable. Hence, I do not say anything. One thing is for sure: The same relationship we have today also existed in our former lives. Because of that past relationship, today it is possible for you to be close to Baba.

Devotee: *Baba, humans need God, but does God also need us, His devotees?*

BABA: If there had been no devotees, God would not have come to

Sri Balasai Baba

earth. He wants them and they want Him. The relationship is mutual. I want to tell you about an event in the life of Sri Krishna. One day Sri Krishna began suffering from painful headaches. The ruler, Narada, eagerly asked for help from all the physicians in the kingdom. But no remedy was effective. After a while, Narada turned desperately towards Krishna, saying, "My Lord, please tell me what might help. I will do everything I can." Krishna asked for some sand, which his devotees had put on their feet. Narada brought the sand, Krishna put it on his forehead and his pains disappeared immediately. The sand of his devotees immediately healed his headache. That is how real love expresses itself. The devotee loves God and God loves the devotee.

This love flows freely from the heart. Love cannot be forced. To melt His heart, you should be like little children, **ready to please and obey Him.**

Devotee: *When my son comes here, I cannot translate your jokes, because then he will not believe that you are a living God.*

BABA: With my jokes I open people up to my teachings. Jokes are door openers. You should listen to them and immediately forget them. God is everything, even the joke. You may not repeat my jokes. Listen to them and then forget them immediately.

God is the embodiment of humor. However, some people think of me as a devil, since I have a sense of humor. **I always say the truth, for I am the truth.**

Laughter keeps us young. We should not be too serious or we will grow old very quickly. A good sense of humor is very important for our happiness.

Devotee: Could we understand your holy secrets, your mysteries?

BABA: Baba is not going to reveal his secrets, since a lot of people would only use them for selfish goals. **The only way to approach me is through love. You should be able to ask me good questions, to grasp my responses and to remember them.** Retain my teachings in your hearts – only there lies true comprehension. I may say a lot of things, but if you do not understand me then everything is just gossip. Those who aim to understand me well will never completely understand my mystery. **You could, however, grow into the mystery through love, more and more love. When you think about God and meditate, recite His holy names, concentrate and direct your attention towards His form. Then you will dive deeper into the mystery of God, forgetting yourself.**

Devotee: I want to come back and see you very soon!

BABA: Why not? The entrance gate is always open to you. If you want to come, then come! If you want to go, then go! Be free! I have a secret to tell you. I do not ask that anybody depend on me. It is enough that you think of me. There are gurus who want to make others dependent on them. This is not good. I want you to become strong, self-reliant people. Rely only on God. **Independence is the best way. Our objective is to live simply and to develop great thoughts.**

BABA'S MOTHER

Devotee: Could you tell us something about your mother? (this interview took place before the death of Sai Baba's mother)

Sri Balasai Baba

BABA: In my eyes, no woman was as beautiful as my mother. Whenever I saw in my youth another woman with a beautiful Sari, I thought, 'only my mother is worth this kind of Sari.' That is how much I loved her. My mother sacrificed everything for her children. As a young woman in her mid-twenties, she lost two sons and her husband within the period of a week.

My mother is a woman with a lot of good characteristics. God has chosen her to give birth to this incarnation. She was widowed at a young age. At that time, we lived next to the temple of Shirdi Sai Baba, in a tiny hut made of bamboo. There were a lot of spiders, rats and snakes. We were the only family of Brahmans here in the district of the temple. Visitors from far away visited the temple and our cottage, where they received delicious food from my mother. Sometimes they borrowed knives and forks, which they did not bring back. When this happened, my mother stood at the altar and scolded God: "Why do you punish me in this manner? Is this right what they do to me? Why do you want me to suffer?" **Throughout her entire life she discussed everything directly with God.**

My mother raised the children alone. Altogether, she gave birth to seven children, of which four survived. She shared her possessions with her children. **God does not choose just anyone to give birth to an incarnation. The person He chooses needs to have divine qualities.**

My mother taught me through a virtuous and exemplary life. Sometimes she punished me hard for things that were against her ethical beliefs. She talked little and stayed in the house all the time. She knew no friendship or contact with others. But anybody who

knocked at her door saw her compassion firsthand.

She spoke four Indian languages and some English. When she moved from Kerala to Kurnool, she did not speak or comprehend one word of Telugu, but within a short period of time she had acquired a broad knowledge of this foreign language and began to teach it to the children of the village. She earned some rupees that way. As a little child, I wanted to learn everything I could from her. I insisted that she teaches me all these languages, which she promised to do. I learned how to read and write very easily.

Although she lived under poor conditions, she shared food with everybody in the house. Even now she keeps this tradition. Our house was always frequented by pilgrims or poor men who had nothing to eat. My mother can only give. She gave her food away, then went back to the corner where nobody could see her. She pretended to get the rest of her food from the pot, even though there wasn't any. I heard the scratching noise of a spoon. But one day I saw that she was only scratching the pot with a spoon; there was no food to be eaten. She wrapped her Sari around her so that nobody could see how slim she was.

Devotee: *How did you react when you discovered that?*
BABA: At first I felt very miserable and had a lot of compassion for her, but I was also very proud of her.

Unfortunately, bad people also knocked at her door to abuse her in her helplessness. Once, she was alone with my dead grandfather. She did not know how to manage the situation. Some men came to her door pretending to help her. They tried to abuse her in her most

Sri Balasai Baba

desperate ways. Although I was only a little boy, I eventually went out to get the necessary burning material. I performed the ritual burning of the dead body.

Since we belonged to the caste of the priests, they often knocked at our door. Some of them wanted to help us by giving us money. My mother never took this money if it came out the hands of a man. So a Brahman priest stepped in front of a picture of God in our hut and laid down the money as a donation.

My mother does not know how much I keep her in my heart. I often try to think how I can make her happier or how I can give her more love, but no matter what I give her or do for her, it will be never enough. Not even a kilogram of gold would match what she has done for me. She sacrificed everything and she carried me nine months in her belly.

She does not see me very often because the door is mostly locked and nobody can enter my room. Not even my mother knows my inner heart, but I am always with her. My heart is big, very big; nobody can understand what my heart is. It burns and almost bursts. I am with you always; I constantly think about how I can make you happier.

Devotee: *(in 1996, to the mother of Sri Balasai Baba): We would like to know when and how you came to recognize that Sri Balasai Baba is a manifestation of God?*
Mother: My husband and I made a pilgrimage to the mountains of Chamundeshwari - close to Mysore, where the divine mother is venerated. As we fell asleep, the Goddess gave us the same kind of dream in which she showed us that she would be incarnated personally through us and that she would give us a child. When we woke up, we

God is responding

told each other of our dreams. We were very happy that the goddess has selected us.

We continued on our pilgrimage. A guru blessed us, telling us that God would incarnate through us. Similar things happened with Katu-Shiva, a holy person we visited. He told us during the blessings that we would give birth to a great human being, a great healer, a great God. When our child was born, we already knew that it was God who had come into our house.

Devotee: *Did you experience any noteworthy moments in the childhood of Baba?*
Mother: When Baba was a baby, he was visited by a king cobra. The cobra wound around him and positioned its head so as to give a shadow to Baba. The shadow formed the shape of an auspicious omen in Indian mythology. It meant that Vishnu had taken a form as the preserver of the world.

As a child, Baba was already beloved by the people who lived around us. We took him everywhere and people showed him a lot of respect. One day, when he was a schoolboy, it was raining very hard. He came home completely dry. Even as a child, he had the power to stay dry in the rain. In childhood, Baba was sensitive. He had the ability to talk to children in their own language. When he called the crows in the language of the crows, all the crows gathered around him. He knows all the languages of all the living birds and animals.

Devotee: *Could you tell us about your husband? What did he do?*
Mother: He was an ardent devotee of the divine mother. He gave mantras and remedies to the people who came to see him. He also gave people Vibuthi – holy ash. The people he treated in this way were healed. For that they venerated him deeply.

Sri Balasai Baba

Devotee: Did your husband materialize anything from nothing?
Mother: No, he did not materialize anything.

BABA'S WORDS

BABA: Did you bring anything to write with? When you are with a divine incarnation, you should always be ready to write down God's words. Otherwise the words are a pure waste of time and energy. Even if you retain the teachings, if you do not pass them on to all humanity, then the words will disappear when you die. If someone had not written down the words of Jesus, then there would not have been a bible. This is how all Holy Scriptures came into existence.

The words of God are pure gem stones – very precious!! The message may not suit you at this moment, but at some point on your life journey, they will heal you, like a valuable medicine. Divine words are like a quickly prepared meal that you carry with you on your journey. You only need to open the lid and eat out of the container. The words of God can be compared to a can of sweets. Eat and enjoy the sweetness. Just as the food nourishes your body, the words of God nourish your soul. If you only keep them in your mind, then they will die with you. But if they are written down in a book, they will provide a treasury for all humanity – even beyond your physical death.

I say everything very briefly; only then is it delicious. If you get a can of sweets and you eat all of them at once, how will you feel? You will have stomach problems. You should only take as much as you can support.

I will only give you what you can support.
What I tell you is always new. We will return to the same topics, but I am not going to repeat myself. Therefore, you should always try to remember all my words.

BAD BEHAVIOR

Devotee: When people come to you, do they often pretend to be something they're not?

BABA: Some people pretend when they come to me. Nice clothing, a soft voice, good behavior. But at home they beat their wife. Outwardly gentle and soft, but inside they are as fierce as a tiger. **Violence belongs to the nature of an animal, not to the nature of a human being. If I am aware of bad behavior, then I will immediately kick the offending person in the buttocks. I cannot tolerate bad habits. Acting like someone else will not work, for I look only into the heart. Sometimes I can be very tough.**

Even with my mother I have to be strict sometimes. Some of my adherents visited her and told her about their problems until she could not stand the pity anymore. She came to me to convince me that I had to do something for these people. I told her that nobody should ever ask another person to speak to Baba for them. Doing so only prolongs suffering.

(The mother of Baba comes into the room and asks if a devotee may touch his feet. Baba refuses.)

Sri Balasai Baba

Here is a practical example of what we are talking about. She tries to convince me. But my decision is made. If I change my mind now, then the same attempt will be made over and over again. But if I give no opportunity, then the person will be unhappy. So what do I do? I say no today, but maybe tomorrow I will call the person to me and he may touch my feet. Then he will be very surprised and happy. **Whatever we do, we have to be aware of the consequences of our actions.**

As long as you blame somebody wrongly, as long as you criticize and hurt others, you hurt God with your behavior. Does it make sense to visit churches and temples to pray to God, then come home and beat your wife? This God to whom you pray at one time in the church, you blame and hurt another time. How then should God see you? Whatever we teach, we must put into practice. If we do not, then we will lose everything. If you do something good and lead a pure life, then you are going to be in heaven. That means that you will live in peace and harmony with yourself and with everybody around you. If you do something evil and you are on the wrong track, then you will have to suffer.

Pride and haughtiness should never sneak into your feelings or thoughts. I will never allow my devotees, at any time, to nourish this kind of disease. Whenever pride and haughtiness darken your door, you have to stop them from entering your heart and clouding your reason. If you fail to do that, then you will remove yourself from me.

In front of you stands a pot with fresh milk. What happens if you add a single drop of poison to it? A single drop will poison the entire milk. **It is the same with your character. If a tiny flaw sneaks in, it will poison all your good characteristics.** There is no reason at all to be haughty or proud, for what you have achieved belongs only to God.

The character of my true devotee needs to be errorless. I cannot tolerate even the smallest weakness, the tiniest defect or mistake. I will cheerfully correct your errors.

Devotee: Baba, how should a person behave towards you when he realizes that he has made a mistake?

BABA: Often when this happens, he feels guilty and does not have the courage to come back. When he gets over it and finds his way back to me, I will look into his face and forgive him.

Nowadays a lot of people speak badly about God and make jokes about Him. Don't get involved in that. Keep yourself away from them. Seek the company of the good and wise! Bad company pulls you down and traps you in an infinite vicious circle: Bad thoughts, bad company, bad deeds and bad karma!

Here we learn that God dwells in everybody. When you come to this place, you should observe my behavior and discover the ways in which I behave. Slowly you will then try to eliminate your unpleasant and negative traits and learn how to behave properly. Gradually, you will be cleansed and you will adopt divine features.

Devotee: I have behaved badly in the past. I recognized this at certain point in my life and then I changed. Do I have to ask God for forgiveness of my past transgressions?

BABA: The fact that you have recognized your errors and changed your life shows that you have already repented and you made up your mind to seek the good path. God is very delighted to see that. God is merciful. He rejoices in small triumphs. He does not punish you for old mistakes for which you have already repented. God is not only here for the good people; He also serves the so-called wicked.

If a person has been mean and bad up to a certain point in his life and suddenly experiences a moment of enlightenment that completely changes his way of living, we should respect that change. Throughout history there have been numerous examples of this. It sometimes happens that a prostitute becomes a saint. In India we say that we should not explore or investigate the past of a holy person or a saint. A saint is a saint; a holy woman is a holy woman. We do not need to ask them about their past. Behind each person there is divinity.

But you have to make the firm promise not to repeat this mistake anymore. God will watch your behavior and forgive you or not, depending on your actions.

God does not listen to empty words. He sees only your past deeds. He looks into your hearts and sees what is there. Nobody can fool God. He is everywhere and He knows everything.

God will strike a balance between your sins and your virtuous actions. The end sum will then decide your future. Be sure that this day will come.

If you are a Christian, respect the Holy Scriptures and follow them. It is not just to criticize them. Try first to understand and to live what is written in them. You can read what will happen at the Last Judgment. You will be measured according to your thoughts, words and deeds. Your love for the Lord will be measured. If you do not give Him one minute of your life, why should he save you? Jesus Christ came on earth and fulfilled his duty. He showed, by his own example, how to lead a life in God. His message and his life was love.

BAD SPIRITS

Devotee: Do bad spirits exist, or are they only imagination?

BABA: Yes, if you believe in God, then you should believe in bad spirits as well. How can you recognize the positive if the negative aspect does not also exist? It is like in a movie. The hero will only appear great through the villain. We always live with contrasts: dark and light, bad and good, plus and minus, male and female. If you believe in God, then you likewise believe in bad spirits.

Devotee: Does that mean that the bad spirits were also created by God?

BABA: Everything originates exclusively from God. However, the lives of the people are decided by their karma, good or bad. If humans do not perform good things in their lives, if they have a bad karma, they become bad spirits. Later, when they have made up for their bad karma and cancelled it out, they will be liberated from their existence as bad spirits. They will be reborn as a human.

Devotee: Can bad spirits occupy humans?

BABA: Yes, but they cannot truly relish anything, because they are without a physical body. They are wandering ghosts.

Devotee: Is there any protection against these bad spirits?

BABA: Yes, if you believe in God, then you will be protected from all evil things, including bad spirits. God will protect you from bad karma, bad thoughts and bad spirits. If you are wrapped in the protection of God, nothing bad can come to you!

Sri Balasai Baba

BALA TRIPURA SUNDARI

Devotee: *Baba is also called Bala Tripura Sundari. What does this mean?*

BABA: Bala Tripura Sundari animates and rules the three energy forms: Brahma, Vishnu and Shiva. Brahma is the creator, Vishnu is the preserver and Shiva is the destroyer. But even they need to ask Bala Tripura Sundari for energy. I am the entire life energy – pure light, formless and nameless. I am the divine power, Shakti. Even the gods depend on this power.

The divine power has incarnated to bless all creatures in the entire universe and to give them the strength they need. One night, the goddess Bala Tripura Sundari appeared to my father and my mother simultaneously in their dreams and announced that she was coming. She said to my mother, "I would like to grow in your belly. You will give me life."

Bala Tripura Sundari is the Shakti Herself. She is the gold bar from which other divinities take their shape. The gods cannot live without Shakti, the female aspect. She is the elementary power, without which there is no existence. Other goddesses are simply aspects of the elemental power.

BHAJANS – SONGS OF PRAISE

Devotee: *Could you please talk about bhajans? I know that they are songs to praise the Lord, but what kinds of effects do they have?*

BABA: Singing bhajans is like group meditation. You call God and God comes. When everybody is gathered, they sing for God and with God. When you are singing the names of God, divine emanations will reach you. The same happens when the people enter the divine temple hospital or the hall of bhajans. Divine radiation and emanations will help them to release their sorrows or diseases and be joyful.

We should never be satisfied with what we have attained. Otherwise there won't be any progress. Try to introduce new songs each day. When you sing old songs, try to sing them differently, from the depth of your heart.

Some people are timid and do not know how to pray to God. Singing praises makes them free and happy. Sing bhajans and think of me. You may not even understand what you sing, but just see what happens. Singing bhajans is a wonderful way of praising God. **While you are singing bhajans, concentrate exclusively on God, not on the people around you!** If you take this advice seriously, then there won't be any competition while you are singing. Bhajan singing is not a contest. It is a spiritual practice to make God happy. Do not pay too much attention to the melody, your own voice, or the microphone. If you do, then the entire exercise is in vain. The singing should originate in the heart and be dedicated to God.

Devotee: *What happens to our soul when we sing bhajans?*

Sri Balasai Baba

BABA: It will be cleansed of all impurities; bhajan singing gives the soul peace. Bhajans are very important. If a devotee sings sweetly and from the heart, then immediately I will fall in love! Singing bhajans also creates an atmosphere of unity among those who sit together and sing.

Devotee: Baba, when I want to sing a certain bhajan in the temple, sometimes another person sings it before me. Does that mean that we are one?

BABA: Yes, this is it. Your souls are merged with the eternal soul.

BLESSINGS

Devotee: Will you bless these prayer beads? I got them from an Indian saint.

BABA: Here we do not bless objects! I bless you. Then all your objects will be automatically blessed. And I bless you with everything good. Every human being on this earth, rich or poor, needs the blessing of God. It would be stupid to believe that one could live without His blessings.

Devotee: Baba, how does your blessing influence my karma?

BABA: My blessing is beneficial for you in various respects. Overall, it gives you the power and the courage you need to look into the eyes of your karma and to face your problems head on.

Although your negative karma still exists, you can better cope with it if you accept my help. If you meet me with an open heart, you will experience a kind of rebirth. This can happen to anyone, regardless of his age. From the moment we meet, you should give everything to me and think always of me. **To think about me, to talk about me, to do something for me – all this builds good karma.** From the moment we meet, you should give everything to me and always think of me. In the mind, you are always with me; all the fruits of your actions come to me.

You should act without expectation. Do not run after material things. They are only there to embellish your worldly existence. There is nothing better than to seek my blessings.

Devotee: *How can we imagine your blessings?*

BABA: Like the air, you cannot see the blessings that I pour over you, but you can feel them. You can feel the blessing of God. It surrounds you like a breath, letting you feel that He is present, helping you on your way. Make efforts for the blessings of God. Be worthy of God's blessing. You should not ask for anything or expect anything from God. Try to love Him. Then things will happen as they should.

BODY

BABA: To ordinary people whose highest goal is not liberation, I always say, "Your body is the temple of God and your soul is like the statue in the inner part of the temple." Take care that your temple is in order. Then the statue will also do fine. You need to take care of both your body and your soul.

Devotee: And the body?

BABA: There is nothing wrong with it. We should cherish it and take care of it. Your body is the temple of God. Therefore, take care of and respect your body. For the realization of God, a sound physical constitution is necessary. If you are physically weak, sick and full of pain, then you will be only concentrated on the body, not on God. I bless you all with good health. You have to sustain and take care of your body. If you let it degenerate, you will become weak and lack the force that you will need in your spiritual future.

However, we should not pay excessive attention to the body. Whether we cover it with jeans, spray it with perfume, wash it with milk, or support it with multivitamins, one thing is for sure: When the time has comes, it needs to go. As surely as the sun sets, we will die.

Nothing in the world should become a habit. Even a massage can become a drug if you do not stop one day. We must live for ourselves, not for an item or an objective.

Devotee: I do not want people to suffer and die.

BABA: All bodies are transitory. Even the body of Baba will go one day. And life is too short, like a soap bubble. What a tragedy it is that humanity does not want to comprehend that everything on earth is ephemeral! By seeking only material happiness, people waste their entire lives. Only God is forever. Even Brahma, Vishnu and Mahesh are ephemeral. Beyond this sustaining, destroying and creative trinity lies the eternal light, beyond existence and non-existence. It does not move; it is ever constant.

BOOKS

Devotee: *Is it useful to read a lot of books?*

BABA: Books only exist to fill your time. What do you get from reading books? Only knowledge of the books, not real, vivid, experiential knowledge.

True spirituality is grounded deep in our hearts. Only there can we experience it. It reveals itself to us through love and devotion to the divine. You cannot study spirituality.

Once you have put into practice what you have read, then you will reach real knowledge, or wisdom. However, it is better to read a good book then to waste your thoughts with useless stuff.

Devotee: *What kind of books should we then read?*

BABA: Chose religious, spiritual, philosophical books. If you read other books, then you are going to confuse your mind. It is true that there is only one God, but different writers have various opinions and views. Their experience is always personal. If you read a lot of spiritual books, then you will learn about the same thing from multiple viewpoints.

We should not read the Holy Scriptures as we would read a novel. We should seek understanding by meditating on the people and the events. If we do not do that, then we will waste our time. Nowadays people read the bible without any profound understanding.

Believe it or not, Baba knows all books, whether he has read them or not. Baba has never read the bible. I just tell about what it is really about. Baba knows the past, the present and the future. You do not need anybody to explain the bible. Read it yourself and try to discover the meaning behind the words. Then you will really comprehend its meaning.

If you really want to understand what is written in the bible, then you should not read more than one page per day. Such is the depth of its content.

Here we do not cite any holy scriptures; we want to convey only practical knowledge. Our goal is to take the love of God to human beings and encourage the love for one's fellow. You need to know that God can be found neither at a pilgrimage site, nor in heaven, nor anywhere else in particular. **God lives in each creature and in each tiny particle of the universe. God is not separated from you. Your duty is to recognize Him in all creatures, to love all and to respect everyone.**

C

CATASTROPHES

Devotee: Baba, sometimes I am afraid when I hear about all the catastrophes that are predicted to destroy a great part of humanity.

BABA: Let the catastrophes come, or not. Don't be afraid. If something should happen, my true devotees will be on the safe side; they won't die. Even after a thousand years, nothing will happen to them. Their souls will be with Baba. Now you are bound to me. In the next life it will be the same. **Your love and devotion will be stronger each time. One day they will be strong enough to let you merge with God.**

CHARITY

Devotee: What should we do if we see that somebody hurts another fellow human?

BABA: You should always do your best. But sometimes it is useful to be mute, deaf and blind. To needlessly intervene in a life of another person is not good. If we truly do not have sufficient time to take care of our own life; why then we should intervene in that of another human?

Sri Balasai Baba

Devotee: *Should we support people who have less money than we do?*

BABA: If we earn money with our work, then we should use a part of it for a good purpose. Even if we only have five euro in our pocket, we can give fifty cents to somebody who needs it. Sharing is not only limited to material goods. We need to be generous in our lives. Being generous is closely linked to liberation.

But we should not help lazy and idle people. Not to help them is the best help. Laziness and crime often go hand in hand. As soon as there is no work, we become lazy. It is easy to become a criminal. We should be aware of that. It is written in the Vedas: Before we take care of others, we must put our own life in order.

Two thousand years ago, some divine teachings of Jesus were disliked. When he saved a sheep, some criticized him, saying that he should not have done so on the Sabbath. Jesus said, "What is wrong with saving a creature in need on the Sabbath? Shall I let something in need die, simply because it is the Sabbath? The Sabbath was created for human beings, not the other way around. Help should be given at any day and at any time. To refuse to help is inhuman and cruel."

Do you know anything about the great Shankara? One day, disguised as a beggar, Shankara knocked on the front door of a woman. He knew that she was very poor, but when she opened the door he asked for a handful of rice anyway. She would have gladly given him something to eat but had no food to offer. For a moment she was perplexed. All of a sudden she remembered that she had put aside some canned food that she could offer him. She went outside, beaming and brought him that food. When he took it he prayed to the goddess Lakshmi that she

pour a blessing of gold upon this woman. Lakshmi did it right away.

Devotee: *Baba, what could we do for your hospital?*

BABA: You have to do your best, without begging for it. The money will be there at the right time. Everyone who contributes to this cause does so for himself, since he creates good karma. But even good karma needs divine grace to become effective.

Devotee: *How can one understand giving and taking?*

BABA: God gives you everything. You should give one-tenth of your income to good causes. It will be dedicated to God. The person who has more gives more, the person who has less gives less. God does not need anything. If you intend to give money for the benefit of humans, then give it to me. Here everything will be used for the well-being of humans and for social projects. **Whatever I get it is not for me, but for all of you.** If you want to do something good, then give me what you can. I will put it to good use!

COMPASSION

Devotee: *Baba, we have to learn a lot from you.*

BABA: Please try. Humanity is in bad condition and I am full of compassion. When I see all the misery in the world, I want to cry. People these days only take care of themselves and maybe their family. But beyond that, they do not have any compassion for other beings. They only care about material concerns, providing for themselves and their families, the education of their children and the like. Their horizon stays very limited.

One day, leaving the ashram on foot, I saw a pregnant dog lying by the side of road. It was unable to move. Its entire body was trembling. It must have suffered greatly, for it tried several times to get up, but soon broke down with weakness. Nobody noticed the animal; nobody cared about her fate.

This situation reminded me of my own mother when she was pregnant - she was very weak and her whole body was trembling, just like the dog. My heart suffers very much when I see that.

Devotee: *Baba, how it is possible that nobody took care of it?*
BABA: I could find no explanation for that in my heavenly dictionary.

CONCENTRATION

Devotee: *How can I see you everywhere and in everything?*
BABA: Whenever you pray for anything, you need my help. If your desire is strong enough, you will surely get the help that you ask for. But nothing will be accomplished without the power of concentration. **Concentration leads to the opening of the inner eye, which can see more than the physical eye.** You can feel the air around you, but you cannot see it. Devotional attention and concentration will help you to see what cannot be seen at first.

Devotee: *How can we develop concentration?*

BABA: What does your son do, when he wants to pass an exam? Study and practice. Nothing will be accomplished if we only try it once. It is not that easy. **Accomplishing anything worthwhile requires patience and practice.**

Even in the spiritual world you need to learn and practice things. If you start to meditate, your thoughts will pull you away to the banalities of daily life. **You need to practice controlling your thoughts.**

As far as meditation is concerned, another beginner's obstacle is the discomfort that your body might be while sitting in meditative posture. It takes time to learn how to sit correctly and comfortably. Your body needs time to learn. If you have stomach pains and you use the pills prescribed by a doctor, you will need time until they become effective. Why would it be different on the spiritual level?

COMMITMENT

Devotee: How do I handle decisions I have made?

BABA *(very strictly)*: As soon as you have decided on something, you have to stick to it, no matter what. Otherwise you are like a monkey, following whatever suits you. The only way to overcome monkey-like behavior is to carry out your conscious decisions mindfully. You should have this attitude: "I will stick to my decision, even if it costs my life." You can decide everything in your life for yourself; you do not need to ask anybody. Sit down at a still place and tune into yourself. Think.

Decide what you will do. Then do what you have decided. Be free. But think about it carefully before you decide, since your future life depends on it.

The human heart always seeks diversity. It is never truly content and it wants always exactly that what it does not have. Thus, we should ignore its mood and instead act on our conscious decisions. If we do not do that, we will always run after new ideas and fall into one quagmire after another. The heart is always unsteady and inconstant. The mind is the same. As long as we feel and think, it will be like that. Our task is to be indifferent towards our ever-changing moods.

CRITICISM

Devotee: What do you think of criticism?

BABA: **Always promote only the good; only speak the good.** It is not right to criticize or judge the religion of others. Who gives you the right to criticize or comment such a great thing as a religion? When you only say good things, then the mistakes of your neighbors will become automatically visible. You do not need to discuss your neighbor's shortcomings. If you condemn others, then you will only reap condemnation yourself. Accept everything with indifference and coolness - this is true enlightenment.

Criticism is a sin; you should never criticize a saint or any other creature. In India, people respect a holy person because they know that he is the representative of God on earth and that he has the knowledge that they need to find God.

But all living beings are creatures of God, not just the saint. God lives in each creature. **If you criticize, you will never advance spiritually. Whatever karmic benefit you derive from your love and devotion will ultimately be lost to criticism and jealousy. Your balance will be zero.** Nobody has the right to criticize another living creature; it is truly a sin. The human being should think before he says something.

Devotee*: Baba, today at the market I was asked where I live and I replied, "in the Balasai Ashram." The shop owner laughed at me. He knows you from childhood and he does not accept your divinity... Why?*

BABA: We should not react to that. Let him talk; let him criticize. His behavior is absolutely normal and human.

Whatever you are doing, ask yourself whether what you intended to do can be integrated with your ultimate goal. Ask if it serves the good. Do not forget your true intentions. Carry out your work as well as you can and stay focused on your goals. Do not deviate from your way, otherwise you will fall into a ditch.

I will tell you a story to illustrate how you should not behave. There was once a laundry man who walked from house to house with his donkey to collect the laundry. One day he thought, "Why don't I purchase a pull cart? With a cart I can more easily transport the laundry than with a donkey." One day he discussed this idea with his son. Together they decided to go to the town to sell the donkey in order to buy a cart.

They went through town walking on either side of the donkey, holding the right and left ear. Some young people passed them and made fun of them, saying, "Look how stupid they are. They walk next to donkey instead of riding on it." Ashamed, they decided that the father should ride on it and the son should run next to it. Then others approached and scowled at them, saying, "The old man should let his son ride on the donkey." The old man agreed and let his son ride on the donkey. A group of people remarked disparagingly: "Look what kind of useless son he is. He should respect the age of the father and let him ride on the donkey." Now both stopped and decided to carry the donkey into the city. But before they could enter the city they had to cross a bridge. Halfway across, they slipped and lost their balance. The donkey slipped away and fell into the river. **Because they listened to the gossip of others, they lost their precious donkey.** This should never happen to you. **Let people complain. Go in the direction upon which you have decided.**

D

DARSHAN

(Note: A darshan is a personal visitation and blessing by a holy person.)

Devotee: *I waited for your darshan, but you did not show up!*

BABA: I have already told you that sometimes I do not give darshans. Sometimes I only give them for a short time. If somebody calls me from afar and needs my help, then I will come to him. Sometimes my body sits in the temple, but my spirit may be somewhere else. Do not worry about that. I am always with you, even if you cannot see me. I am always with you.

Devotee: *Sometimes you give only a very brief darshan. Why?*

BABA: When Baba does not come into the temple, this means that his presence is not needed, or that somewhere on earth there is somebody who needs Baba urgently or yearns for him more than the people in the temple. Even at this moment, while he is sitting here, talking to you, he is at many other places. You should never think that God sits only with you and talks to you; this would be very silly. God is here, but He is simultaneously at thousands of other places in the universe.

Sri Balasai Baba

DEATH

Devotee: And what about death?

BABA: At the moment of death, you need to be completely focused on God. This you should practice very early, for at the moment of death it will be very difficult to keep your mind on God without being distracted. You need to prepare yourself for what will come. Why do you think we send our children to school when they are young? We prepare them for life. We must similarly prepare ourselves for death by seeking God now, not later.

Devotee: Why is that?

BABA: There are different kinds of pain that could accompany death. The greatest and most terrible pains in life are the pains of birth and the pains of death. If you manage to concentrate intensely on God and forget yourself, even while you are dying, then you will merge with God. Then the body will simply fall off, like a piece of clothing.

You are being persecuted by Yama, the god of death. Yama does not miss an opportunity to drag you to his side and to take you to hell. He is very powerful and does not wait till you are old and ready to die. **He is always near you.** Therefore you should dedicate yourself to God at an early age. Do not wait until you are sixty years old. At the age of sixty you have already lost the physical and mental power that you need to carry out spiritual practices. Your muscles and your body become weak. It is never too late to return to God, but it is very strenuous to do so late in life.

God is responding

Devotee: *If we help somebody when he dies, can we help prepare him to meet with God?*

BABA: How can anybody else intervene on behalf of a dying person? If a woman is hungry and her husband eats a plate of rice and vegetables, will be the woman's stomach be full? Of course not!

It requires a lot of luck and good karma to think about God. We must constantly practice saying the names of God. To remember God when facing death is not easy; it requires a lot of practice. Do you know why we give our children the names of God? We do it because it is important for a dying person to hear himself calling out the holy names of God as he dies.

The body has to endure a lot of aches and pains. We must endure times when our thoughts are everywhere but with God. We must use our lives to prepare ourselves for that final moment, when we must focus our thoughts on God.

Devotee: *I once accidentally swallowed a candy and could not breathe. I could only perceive the fear of death and could not think of Baba.*

BABA: You should be grateful for this experience. Now you know how it will be when you die. You know that you need more spiritual practice if want to be able to think of God at the moment of death. You have learned this lesson, but you did not have to die to learn it! For that you should be grateful to God. He has assumed the form of the man who hit you on the back to dislodge the candy. **God does not need to come personally; He can help through any form.**

Devotee: *Please talk to us about life after death. What happens to the soul after we die?*

BABA: Life is like a knife. If somebody puts a knife in your hand, you can use it to cut vegetables or you can use it to cut your own throat. **Life is in your hands! If you do good things, you will accumulate good karma and thereby have a good life.** The life you now live will determine the quality of your next life. Better efforts, better fruits. Development from one lifetime to the other will happen slowly, slowly, slowly. If you stick to your goals and do good things in your life, you will become one with God. Until then, the circle of life and death will continue.

DETACHMENT

Devotee: Baba, can I have attachments?

BABA: Do have good relations, but don't be bound. Attachment is illusion - detachment is solution. Be free!

Once you reach a state of detachment from worldly affairs, you will reap great happiness. You should not waste one moment in laying your life down at my feet. Your thoughts should be focused completely on me. You should always think: **"How can I merge with God? How can I conquer His heart? How can I get His grace? How can I make Him happy?"**

Within every desire and every thought lies the seed for your next birth. Suppose you become very attached to a certain person in your life and you continue to think of him alone, even when you die. When you are reborn, you will be bound to help this person

God is responding

throughout your life. You will thereby experience only suffering. Even if that person attains liberation, you will not be happy. You will lose your sense of purpose. You will seek something without knowing what you are longing for. You will become depressed without knowing why. Live so that you can think of God in your final moment. Then your liberation will be certain.

If your body is here, but your thoughts are with your family, friends and worldly possessions, then you have to deal with a few more reincarnations to satisfy your wishes. Only then will all your thoughts be focused on God. Only when you devote every breath to Him, He can guide you. Once you have moved into my heart, I have to take care of you completely. That is my task. This is a golden opportunity for you to merge with God. The goal of human existence is to become one with God. You should make this your own personal goal.

Once you know that there is a pure mountain spring available, why then you want to bathe in a swamp? God is the spring and swamp is the material world, the society that wants to get hold of you. You have to be careful not to fall back into its claws. **It takes effort and willpower to stay with God.**

In life, we must welcome problems and obstacles. How can you expect to explore the depths of life if you always stay on the surface? Life is an adventure! Live it. Be courageous. Be fearless. Courage is the prerequisite for success. Baba is always with you.

Devotee: *Baba, I feel strange here. Everything is new and different. I long for my wife and my children.*

BABA: We are all foreigners on this earth. We are like tenants in a rented house. We never know when we will have to get out. We are born and one day we are going to die. That is one hundred percent certain. In this material world, nothing is eternal. Therefore we should not be attached to anybody or anything. We are born alone and will die alone. Nobody can accompany us. In the moment of death we cannot take any worldly items with us. We came to earth with empty hands and with empty hands we will leave the world again.

So why should we attach such importance to such fleeting things? Practice the spiritual values of tolerance, righteousness, truth, non-violence and love for all creatures. To only take care of one's own well-being is very selfish; we must include God in our lives.

Devotee: *I am only a human! I make many mistakes.*

BABA: That is no excuse. All humans make a lot of mistakes, from the moment they are born. Try to counteract them and develop love for all creatures. To love one's husband or wife is not wrong, but to fail to love others is not good. If we cannot love others, then we should at least yearn to do so.

You said you are only a normal human being, but you must realize that you are something special. You are God. God acts through you, but you do not fully realize this fact. Do not think that you are an ordinary human being. Know that you are something special. You can translate your shortcomings into good qualities.

You come to earth alone. You will likewise leave it alone. You presently live only for yourself, for your wife and for your children. This is a pity. It is a spurious attachment. Outwardly we can be attached, but inwardly we should always be detached. We do not need to suffer

when our relatives are not with us. **Only God can protect you!**

The good and the bad play hide and seek throughout our lives. We never know when the one or the other will attack. We should therefore not worry, but stay detached from our surroundings. Let things happen. Nothing is eternal. Good times come, bad times go. Bad times come, good times go. Therefore, do not suffer. You are immortal; you are God. A drop of water that gets disconnected from the ocean and jumps into the air is not separated from the ocean. The ocean and the water droplet are one.

If you identify with yourself, you will be trapped in illusion. You will not know who you really are. I love and bless you. **Remember that you are never alone! God always stands behind you! Pray to Him.**

If you do not reach God in this life, then you will reach Him in another life. But on the way to Him, you will find true happiness and joy. God will fill you with His love.

DEVOTEES

Devotee: Did you come to earth for the devotees?
BABA: I came to this earth for my devotees.

Devotee: What is the difference between a disciple and a devotee?
BABA: I do not have any disciples. A guru has disciples. A guru teaches the disciple a mantra according to his discretion. The disciple serves his

Sri Balasai Baba

guru throughout his entire life. 24 hours a day, he does everything for his guru. He even washes his underwear.

But my devotees often come only once in their lives! They come to get my blessings for the fulfillment of their wishes. They arrive by bus with the return ticket already in their pocket. They only stay for a few hours. They want their wishes to be quickly fulfilled so that they can immediately travel back.

Devotee: *What can a devotee do?*

BABA: If I were a devotee of God, I would always think about what I might do for God. Eyes, ears and nose should be considered gateways to the heart.

Devotee: *Please help me not to forget all that.*

BABA: You should not ask me to help you not to forget it, but rather, to help you make efforts so that I do not need to repeat it again.

Devotee: *What is a true devotee?*

BABA: Somebody who has devoted his life to God can be called a true devotee. A lot of people will come to Baba and behave as if they were the perfect devotee. They want to get something for themselves and they assume that through my blessings, all their wishes will be fulfilled. They make promises that they do not keep. They think that they are being quite smart. They think that God won't notice their deceit. **But I see their inner hearts. Every hidden thought, every motive and every secret intention lies open before me. I know every corner of their feelings. I can see into the hearts of humans. Nobody, however intelligent he might be, can ever deceive me.**

Outwardly, I might give the impression that I will fulfill your desires. I listen carefully and lovingly, indulging your requests and complaints, **but inwardly I have already made up my mind. Without exception, whatever the divine will decides upon will happen.**

Even those who give the impression that they are close to me cannot make me alter my decisions. I act according to their own karmic histories. If they have created something good, then they will get something good. If they have done something bad, then they will get something bad. **Living close to me does not mean that people will be acquitted of their deeds. Closeness to me results from good karma in the last life. But it is necessary to do more good things to be able to stay close to me. If your positive karma is used up and you have not accumulated more merit, you will no longer be near me.**

DEVOTION

Devotee: *How can we practice our devotion?*

BABA: Devotion should stem from the your innermost part of your heart. It comes from deep within yourself - not in the brain, but in the heart. Suppose you go for a walk in the park and see a woman passing near you. Could you approach her and order her to love you? How would she react? I cannot force you to love me and to be devoted to me. However, you could try to generate feelings of devotion within yourself by visiting sacred sites and to talking to people who have experienced God. Reading spiritual books will also help.
Already you now feel something like love towards me. Go further.

Sri Balasai Baba

Nurture your feeling. Your love will bring you closer and closer to me. I will love you and make you happy.

Everything comes from God. If you are joyful today, think, 'It is a gift from God.' If you are sad tomorrow and you suffer, think again, 'It is a gift from God.' Always be grateful to God. Suppose that today you eat rice with three kinds of vegetables. You are very happy. If tomorrow you only drink a glass of water, thank God for the glass of water He gives you to quench your thirst. If you think and act in this way, then you are free.

Devotee: *Is devotion only possible when I have deep feelings for God? I am not someone who usually has deep feelings. Is there a special recipe for me?*

BABA: **Not everyone can walk on the spiritual path. You may build up your own relationship with God in your own way.** Even if you perform good deeds mechanically, God will be very happy about it. Sing bhajans and think of me. That kind of practice is sufficient for me. You do not even to comprehend what you sing. Sing and observe what will happen.

Devotee: *To love you is very painful because I cannot always see you!*

BABA: There are two kinds of pain. One you feel when you hurt yourself and the other is called Badha - the sweet pain of spiritual love. The existence of the entire universe depends on it. To suffer for God is good; it brings you closer to Him.

Devotee: *For the sake of God, I have renounced smoking. What will happen if I start again?*

BABA: If you have given something up for God, you never want it back. If you start to smoke again, you will break a contract with God.

That is a great sin. Negative feelings, sicknesses and bad habits will come back to you. These problems will be connected to your smoking habit. Additionally, if you forsake your promise, I will expose you to public ridicule. **Therefore, think very carefully about what you do and what you promise.**

DHARMA

Devotee: What is the meaning of dharma?

BABA: Dharma means duty. If you are good devotee of God, you will venerate Him, bring Him sacrifices and thus fulfill your dharma as a devotee of God.

Let us consider marriage as an example. To love her husband and to take care of him is the dharma of the wife. To take care of the children is the dharma of the parents. To obey the parents and to respect them is the dharma of the children. When you are sick, it is your dharma to go to the physician and it is the dharma of the physician to help you.

Dharma is for those who are on the good path. Godless and dishonest people do not worry about dharma. A criminal will be automatically punished by dharma, by society and by the law. He will ultimately find himself in prison. Whoever obeys dharma will think about how he can do something good.

Devotee: My son is currently living a loose life. Shall I pray for him?

BABA: As his mother, you can pray for the well-being of your son, thus fulfilling the dharma of the mother. As a mother, it is your dharma, your duty, to bring him on the right path. If a person has a lot of good characteristics, but does not do his duty, than he will not be a good person. It is similar to a giant pot full of water. If there is a tiny hole in the pot, then through it all the water will disappear.

To say good things is the duty of a master. Whether you listen to him or not is your problem. If you do not follow rules and regulations, then you will violate the dharma and the punishment of God will be exacted. **I offer you my help. Take it, for God is the only one who can help you. His admiration and love is always there for you. He will forgive you, if you ask Him.**

A lot of people tell me about their problems and physical pains. I advise them to go to the doctor so that the cause of their problems can be determined. "No!" they say. "You take away the pains!" I reply: "No, no," It is your dharma to go to the doctor. He will find out about the causes of your sufferings and prescribe a treatment. Thereafter you can come to me and I will give you my blessings." We should always obey our dharma.

Devotee: *What is your dharma? What is your duty?*

BABA: To teach the humans to love each other. The divine incarnation comes only to fulfill his duties. Because of the infinite love he has for his creatures, he takes a human form and behaves like a human being. When society decays, when hardly any love or righteousness exists on earth, God sacrifices Himself for the benefit of the humanity.

He comes only to give. He won't take anything from anybody.

God is responding

You should do the same. Give your life to humanity and do only good. This is your duty, for which you should not expect anything in return. When you do something good, your reward will come, but you should not anticipate it. You should not do good only to reap the rewards of good karma.

Devotee: *Isn't it boring for you to say the same things over and over?*

BABA: I do my duty 24 hours a day, every day. My life is a pure routine. I do not belong to anybody. I am public property.

Devotee: *What is duty?*

BABA: Fulfillment of your duty is the purpose of your life. A duty-bound life is paramount. Without duty, disorder reigns supreme.

Devotee: *So a sense of duty is the way to bring discipline into our life?*

BABA: **It is the light of life.** Duty is the lamp that shines on the wick of efforts, producing the flame of faith. Duty is the clear way to illuminate the map of peace and of prosperity. The wise man fulfills his duties. A person with a sense of duty finds his place in society secured. **A person with a sense of duty feels physically and mentally able to meet any obstacles. His inner voice always reminds him not to neglect his duties. Whoever fulfills his duty will be rewarded accordingly.**

The garden of God is open to everybody, regardless of caste, religion, color or gender. Anybody has the right to enter the garden. But God cannot be blamed for the action or inaction of an individual. Negligence of your duties is no one's fault but your own.

Once a king tested the responsibility of his three sons. He had

Sri Balasai Baba

become very old and wanted to give ruling power to one of his sons. The three sons gathered in the private room of the king. The king addressed them and spoke: "I am giving you a task to perform in order to prove your sense of duty."

Each of the three sons was given a statue made of sandalwood. Their task was to cross a river from one bank to the other without getting the statue wet. Each of the three princes jumped into the river and crossed to the other bank. Two brothers were reckless with their statues and did not take care to keep them dry. They put them unwrapped into the pockets of their royal robes as they crossed the river, so their statues became wet. But the third brother's statue stayed completely dry. Aware of his duty, he had wrapped the statue in a thick cloth and fixed this bundle at the upper part of his throat. While crossing the river he had tried with all his might to keep his throat over the water so that his well-wrapped sandalwood statue would not touch the water. As a result of his determination and sense of duty, this third son successfully passed the test.

The king gathered his three sons around him. The three statues were put in front of him. The third son's statue was completely dry and uninjured. The king was impressed by his youngest son's sense of duty and declared in front of the entire court that the third son would immediately begin ruling over the country.

I will teach you what you need to know. This is my task. Your task is to listen to me and to comprehend my words. I am here to teach you good things and to help you out of the darkness, but you should provide me an empty vessel into which I can put my teachings. Anger, pride, jealousy, envy and egoism are your biggest enemies. They act as poison, dragging you down and killing you mercilessly. You should not permit them to rule over your life. If you want to receive the blessings of God, try to eliminate your bad characteristics.

Try to please God, so that He pours his grace over you. Getting the blessings of God is not easy. He observes you carefully. Try to put into practice what Baba says. Try to be an example to others. If they ask you what Baba is about, then you should be able to respond, but it is even better to make your life an example of the teachings I have given you. Put my words into practice.

Whenever you offer and scarify anything to God, do it with a joyful heart. Do not make sacrifices to God with a joyless and greedy feeling. You should do everything with a full and joyful heart. Otherwise, your spiritual practices will not bring you joy; they will only leave you irritated and angry.

If you touch your partner without love and affection, then you will cause him to be angry. However, if you touch each other with feelings of love and happiness, you will be blissful. It is the same with God.

DIFFICULTIES

Devotee: *How can I get out of my problems?*

BABA: Let the problems come and go! They suddenly appear because they are mandated by our karma. Let them be there! Do not worry about them. Be free! Do good, speak good and think good thoughts - that is the way to God. Life is truly tragic, but most people do not want to wake up from this tragic world. They rather love the swamp in which they are stuck. What is the difference between the material life and the spiritual life? Nothing in the material world is permanent. Only on the spiritual level we can find the eternal und unchangeable.

When affliction overcomes you, you must think: "O God, how graceful you are. This affliction belongs to you alone." You can overcome your suffering. If joy and happiness are with you, then you need to think: "O God, how graceful you are. This happiness belongs to you alone." Remember always that everything is God and everything belongs to God. Nothing is yours. Then the life on earth becomes simple and bearable. Even death will not make you afraid.

Devotee: *The humans come to you with problems.*

BABA: The humans only come to me so that I solve their problems. They don't really care about me; as soon as their life is in order again, they forget me. This is a pity. Very often they criticize me because I have not helped them. But this does not matter to me. I am the sun and you are people who stand on earth and look upon the sun. If you want to spit on the sun, what will happen? You will only end up spitting on yourself.

Devotee: *And how should I deal with my inner enemies?*

BABA: Everybody is born with inner fiends, like pride, egoism, envy, or jealousy. Whatever a man accomplishes in the course of his life, he thinks that it is by virtue of his own work - the skills and his talents of which he is proud.

But in the life of each human, there will come a day when difficulties and obstacles appear to be insurmountable. Suddenly, the man does not know how to advance anymore. This is the point at which he turns toward the divine and finally perceives that it is not himself but God who is responsible for the outcome of events. Now the man sees that God is responsible for all things and that without God, the man is nothing. But we do not have to wait for that moment to come; we can realize it ourselves.

If man believes that he alone copes with his problems, fears and sorrows, then God will only watch. He will leave the man alone. But if man dedicates himself to God, if he opens himself up, if he integrates God into his life, if he dedicates to God all his actions and gives to God all the fruits of his labors, if he shows full dedication towards God, then God will be immediately ready to reveal Himself, to carry the burden of humanity and to grant help in all of life's problems.

It is not my duty to solve your problems. When you pray to me, then I will give you the necessary power to solve them. I will guide you, but you have to act yourself. The wishes of human beings are endless. I have not come to fulfill all of them. I will satisfy some of them. That will plant faith and confidence in your heart. Then, slowly, I will show you the way to unity with God. I will say, "Come, come! This is the right way."

DREAMS

Devotee: *If we dream of a saint, a guru or an avatar while we are asleep, are we in unconscious contact with God?*

BABA: In dreams, any relationship with God is possible.

Devotee: *Some dreams of you, Baba, I simply cannot understand.*

BABA: You do not have to understand. Be happy that I appeared in the dream.

1. Meditation is a way of accessing God.
2. Hoping for God is service to God.
3. Dreams of God are direct connections to God.

E

EARTH

Devotee: *It is strange that we fly to the moon when we know so little about Mother Earth.*

BABA: There are still so many places on earth that have not been discovered by anybody. They are not mentioned in the atlas. There are not only many undiscovered places, but we also have much to learn about many species of plants and animals.

Humanity should first concentrate on small achievements before moving on. Instead of leaving the earth, it would be better for people to concentrate on dealing with all these uncured diseases. For all our advanced medicine, we often seem incapable of true healing. Nowadays, doctors seem more interested in their own material success than in healing.

EFFORT

Devotee: Baba, why can't big wishes, like liberation, for instance, be fulfilled immediately?

BABA: Unfortunately it is not that easy. For this we have to take action. But there are ways that lead you to me more quickly.

Devotee: And what are these ways?

BABA: **You need to work on the refinement of your character. You need to destroy your little ego and try to do things God might like.**

Devotee: Could God not destroy our ego?

BABA: If God had done everything for you, where would you be then? It is very easy to say, 'God will yet destroy my ego.' You have to give your best, so that God blesses you and supports you in your efforts. **If God sees that everything you do is to make Him happy, His heart will melt and He will pour His silent blessings over you.**

Without divine grace, there is no healing. Without effort there is no grace. Both are necessary. Therefore, do your best and let God do the rest.

When somebody comes to me for the first time, I tell that person that I dwell in him. Once you have found me, you should never leave me, for it will be a long time before you will have another opportunity to be with me.

God is responding

Suppose, for example, that you are sitting in the front row of the temple. Everybody knows you and respects your position. If you do not stay there, somebody else will take this place and relish its advantages - you will be out and you will have lost your chance. If you try to come back after a long time, people will treat you like a foreigner and push you to the last row.

It is the same with God. When you have found God, you need to attach to Him and never forsake Him. Try to think of Him and keep Him in your heart always. Otherwise you will have lost your chance.

To become one with Him, ask yourself: What is God? What kind of qualities does He possess? How can I merge with Him? How can I win His heart? How can I get His blessings and His grace? For this you can employ your ego, since it will be focused on God, not only on yourself. Do not let your ego focus your energies on yourself! If you start thinking: "Who am I? Why am I here? Why so many rebirths?" you will get lost in difficulties and rebirths. You will suffer tremendously.

Thinking about God alone is the shortest and most joyful way to your ultimate objective. To merge with God, you need to be disciplined. 24 hours a day you must think of Him, see His form and have His name on your lips. If you are completely dedicated to God, then it will be He who thinks, speaks and acts. You will become His instrument. All the fruits of your actions will belong to Him; you will be completely free.

Devotee: How can I work on my character?

BABA: Do not waste any time! **Work on your character by constantly watching your thoughts, words and deeds. Think, say**

and do only good things. You will have to bear the consequences of your thoughts, words and actions.

Do not waste your life by sitting around doing nothing. Give meaning to your life by doing something good. Let it be a service to God. Use all your skills and abilities for the betterment of humanity. If you live only for eating, drinking, sleeping and earning money, then it is better to die. **Wherever you are, feel my hand in your hand. Think, feel, speak and act with the awareness that God walks at your side. Then you are on the right track.**

Devotee: *What if I expend a lot of effort, but still my negative tendencies remain?*

BABA: In this Balasai Baba incarnation, God has decided that humans will be led to the good through his blessings and divine instructions. If somebody's actions are 80% good and 20% bad, then he has the chance, by virtue of his own efforts and my blessings, to become a 100% good person.

My promise goes even further. I will still liberate people who do not make an effort to transform their own negative tendencies. I will give liberation to those who are not my devotees. The knowledge that God is present in each of you should inspire you to do only good things and to avoid evil.

On the spiritual path, it is crucial to pursue one singular goal with which you can align all your thoughts and energies. When we work for a goal, we will certainly reach it someday. There is a big difference between meeting God and merging with God. You have already reached Him, but the next step is to become one with Him.

Such practices as yoga or pranayama *(breathing exercises)* could help us to think about God, for it is the goal of all humans to become one with God.

If you have a goal in life, you should relentlessly pursue that goal. If you want to fly from Mumbai to Frankfurt, you are not inclined to have an intermediate stop in Rome or London. Your destination is Frankfurt. Similarly, your goal is to merge with God. When you gain divine powers through spiritual experience, you should not misuse them. The best thing is not to worry about them, but to continue on your path. If you want to do something with them, then you shall do something good in the name of God. Your intention and your efforts should be always directed towards your goal.

ENLIGHTENMENT

Devotee: What is enlightment?

BABA: Enlightment is nothing other than the realization of God. When you do not recognize anything as not God - as soon as anything besides God does not exist for you - that is enlightenment.

Devotee: If you are no longer attached to an ego, is this the state that is known as enlightenment or liberation?

BABA: As long as the soul stays in the body, complete liberation is impossible. A little breath will always be left over. As long as the body exists, a tiny breath of ego sticks to it. Before merging with God, the veil of ignorance needs to be removed. The ego stands in the way. It is like eye surgery. First there is a little pain. After that, you can see.

Devotee: How can I recognize a truly enlightened person?

BABA: A true enlightened soul shows love, compassion and mercy towards all living creatures. The truly enlightened person does not make any distinction between rich and poor, well and sick, beautiful and ugly. For him everyone is the same, for God sees Himself in everybody. An enlightened person does not differentiate between praise and rebuke; he accepts everything with indifference. He does not react when you spit in his face, nor does he react when you blame or praise him. Whatever he encounters, good or bad, he accepts it with indifference.

A truly self-actualized human being will never come and say: "I am enlightened - I am a sage." People are going automatically going to learn by his behavior. When Jesus was blamed and insulted, when the crown of thorns was pressed on his head, through all his pains and sufferings, he only uttered this: "Father, forgive them, for they know not what they do!"

Devotee: Will the experience of enlightenment only come if the body and the spirit are purified and the breath of life flows freely?

BABA: Regarding breathing, if the temple is in good condition, then the sanctuary of the temple will be secured. Without body there is no soul and without soul there is no body. Now I want to ask you: What would be the benefit of attaining your goal?

Devotee: We would experience that God is everything.

BABA: That is good. The truth is that a lot of people simply want to get the ability to predict the future, to walk over the water, or to fly through the air.

Here is an illustrative story: There were two people. One of them had been practicing for twenty years to walk on the water. They met at the same spot by the side of a river. The one who could walk over the water said to the other, "For more than twenty years I have been practicing to walk on water." He walked on the water. The other was not impressed. He paid a boatman half a rupee to take him across the river. When the boat reached the other side of the river, the man who had taken the boat asked the other, "What have you learned over the last twenty years - only to walk on the water? For that you have sacrificed twenty precious years of your life? What a pity! During this time you should have dedicated your thoughts to God."

ENVY

Devotee: *Where does envy come from?*

BABA: When love grows, envy and desire also grow. There is also the selfish desire to possess God for oneself. **You, the devotees, should not become envious, but instead concentrate on my happiness and that of others.** You should always try to ensure the happiness of others. God belongs to everybody; there is no reason for jealousy and envy. God has a lot of women and of men. The envious ones burn themselves.

Devotee: Baba, when you hold my hand and give me a lot of attention, certainly some people will experience jealousy and envy. If I had to watch you heap such attention on others, then I would become envious. How can I get rid of such envy?

Sri Balasai Baba

BABA: Simply think that whoever is enjoying favorable circumstances must have good karma. Envy can be employed positively. Do not be angry with that person; instead labor to do good things and thus attain good karmic status. Promote only the good.

Baba is available to everybody. Nobody can own me. I am here to give my love and joy to everybody. If somebody has the opportunity to be close to Baba and to have some time to talk with him, then you should not allow yourself to be jealous. Be happy for her or him. You have to be absolutely convinced that the time or opportunity will also come to you. Try to think positively, always. **Do not allow envy or hatred to possess you.**

I am like a physician who takes care of the emergency cases before all other cases. As long as there is a patient is in the emergency room, the physician must treat him first. Other patients might come every day, but the physician must first take care of the emergency case. You should always know that whatever Baba does, he does it for a good reason.

Why did you come here? You want to overcome all the negative tendencies that you have carried since your birth. Anger, pride, jealousy, envy and egotism are bad characteristics. Some people on the spiritual path think that they venerate God. But God simply laughs, because through their angry, jealous, envious and egoistic behavior they venerate only Satan.

Do you know what a tamarind is? It is a sour fruit. You can wash it as often as you want, but it will never lose its sour taste. You are not tamarinds; you are humans! As humans, you can learn to control your

God is responding

tongue. For with your words you can kill life or create life. By being friendly, you do not lose anything. **Try to develop a generous heart and to meet other people with kindness.** If you are not ready for that, why are you here in the ashram?

There are a lot of people who are not on the spiritual path, but who have many good characteristics. What will happen if they come here and see so many jealous hearts? They will get the wrong impression of the spiritual path.

You might be here for some time, then go back into the world. Behave in the same way there that you behave here, otherwise your relatives will think: "They were close to a divine incarnation, but they have not learned anything." Then I will get a bad reputation. Thus I beg you: I should not get a bad reputation because you are unable to put my words into practice.

Envy, jealousness, anger and pride act like a poison. If you do not decide to eliminate these tendencies, then they will annihilate you. My love is thousand times stronger than the love of a mother, but do not think: "I would like to talk personally with Baba." Do not be jealous of someone else who has had a personal interview with Baba. Be aware of envy and jealousy! Do not give these negative feelings any space, or you will fall immediately into a deep hole, where jealousy and envy will kill you.

Examine your jealousy; search relentlessly for its cause. Then release it or annihilate it gradually. In Christianity, we have the cross as the symbol that the ego should be destroyed. Lay your ego at the feet of Baba; he will take it away. Instead of being jealous of somebody, it is better to pray in the following way: **"O God, please present me the same confidence and let me come closer to Thee."** Then no jealousy will be generated.

Devotee: *I do that, but I do not have the feeling that Baba does anything.*

BABA: How do you know that? If you possess a lot of something, then you won't notice a gradual reduction. Your ego is like a big lake from which you must skim off a cup of water every day.

You need to be patient and trust in Baba's help. Every man has weaknesses and strengths. Everyone behaves badly from time to time. Recognize your mistakes, examine them and decide not to repeat them anymore.

EVIL

Devotee: *Baba, is the current state of the world bad?*

BABA: There is also something good in this world, otherwise you would not be able to perceive happiness and joy. Thanks to the saints, rishis and yogis who live in constant communion with God, the joy and the good still exist.

Without the sacrifices of these people, the world would be in a terrible state. Life can be very tragic and horrible.

Many of the people who come to me do so on account of a guilty conscience. If they look into my face, they confess their crimes and ask me for forgiveness. My heart has died many times while listening to these stories of crime.

We now find ourselves in an era in which three-quarters of the population are attracted by the temptations of sex, alcohol, drugs and cigarettes. It is an age of distraction and temptation. Do you remember when Jesus prayed alone and Satan appeared and tried to seduce him? As soon as we try to concentrate on God, Satan comes in and tries to distract us from our good intentions. Today he possesses more power than ever.

Devotee: Were conditions always this bad?

BABA: There has always been temptation, but things were never as bad as they are today. *(To an older devotee:)* You are older than fifty. Recall society of 50 years ago and compare it with today's culture. Then you will immediately know what I mean by the decline of the dharma.

On the other hand, it has never been so easy to be close to God as it is now. In former times, people had to meditate for a thousand years just to get God's blessing for a fraction of a second. Now, because evil is so rampant, God needs to do more to protect his devotees. He loosens the rules of the game for their sake, to ward off evil.

Devotee: If everything is God, then does Satan really exist?

BABA: Even a short moment is sufficient to let this evil companion enter into your life. If you think of Satan, then Satan will appear. He will take as much space in your life as you give him. Why do you permit yourself to think of him? It is much better to direct your concentration towards God. The duty of Satan is to keep you away from the

Sri Balasai Baba

spiritual path. Your duty is to escape from him!

Devotee: *How can we destroy the evil in a human being?*

BABA: The evil within a human being can only be destroyed by exposing it to the light. That is the work of Baba. He drags everything into the divine light. The ego experiences this as a very painful act. However, it represents the chance to unite with the Higher Self – with God. Former divine incarnations came to annihilate the bad and the evil. But in doing so, the good was also destroyed, since no human being is totally evil. Each human being carries within it the potential for good as well as evil. There are differences in the percentage, but nobody is hundred percent good or bad.

The Balasai incarnation came to earth to annihilate the evil in human beings and to change it into hundred percent good. Nowadays, God does not kill the human being, but only the evil within him. The divine incarnation Rama killed the big, mighty king of demons. That was a great deed. But to transform such a creature into a mighty king of good is an even greater deed.

Devotee: *I have trouble judging whether a person is positive or negative.*

BABA: Both aspects are always present. Take the good and leave the other part. **One can see the good or the bad in everything. It is up to you - what you see will then come back to you.**

God alone has access to the heart of a human. If you stand in front of someone and only look at his appearance, you do not know what is hidden behind him. He might be charming, attractive and elegant, but in reality he might treat his wife sadistically. An animal always attacks its foes directly. But a human being is capable of speaking nicely about someone in his presence, then attacking him when his back is turned or to grumble about this person when he turned his back towards him. You need make up your mind to discard all inhuman and satanic behaviors.

Devotee: *Does everything bad in the world also originate from God?*
BABA: God only wants the good!

Devotee:Why does Baba always talk about our bad characteristics?
BABA: There is always a struggle between good and evil, light and darkness. In this world of appearances, we need to learn to perceive the darkness and strive for the light with our power of discrimination. Former incarnations of God killed bad people, but our task is to bring out the good of each human.

By speaking about your bad characters, I will bring up bad things that have been previously suppressed. **If we hide that which is bad within ourselves, we will become sick and depressed. As soon as we speak out about our concerns, a burden falls from us and we feel relieved.**

Something always wants to get out of our body, whether it is breath, tears, sweat, urine or excrement. You must do away with these waste products. Similarly, as soon as something bothers you, it is best to sit down in a quiet corner in front of a picture of Baba, or speak to Baba in your heart. Tell him everything that matters to you and prevents you from being joyful and happy!

Devotee: *Baba, why did you create evil at all?*

Sri Balasai Baba

BABA: Wherever you look, you will see contrast, polar opposites. Even our language possesses the right words to express unequivocally these contrasts: sinner and saint, bad and good, dark and light, materialistic and spiritual and so on. Since you live in a bipolar world, you see good and bad everywhere. Where there is light there is also shadow; where a mouse exists, the cat is not far away. Everywhere, even on this spot, you find good and bad. The supposed contrasts exist only for those who are not enlightened, but not for God. For Him everything is one. He does not see the good and the evil; He only sees one thing, namely only Himself in creation. Between the good and God there is no difference. Without Satan you could not understand the value of God. Those who are afraid of Satan will automatically find their way to God.

Devotee: Why does evil seem to govern the world?

BABA: Everybody runs after money and this is very bad. Beware of that. If we always think about money and wealth, then we will fall into a very deep ditch. When we are blessed with money and goods, it is good to think that we have enough to live comfortably. When we do not have anything, then it is good to thank God for the glass of water that He gives us every day. Be thankful for what you have.

Everything in the life of a human happens according to his karma. In his destiny it is written down whether he will be wealthy or not. This means that money will either come, or it will not. You do not need to run after it. Have trust – even about money. If you include God in everything that you think and do, then He will give you what you really need.

God wants only the good. When you go into a restaurant, you want to

God is responding

enjoy a tasty meal; you do not want to eat refuse from the dustbin. God is beauty and happiness - He is not interested in disgusting and sad things. You should try to please and flatter Him. Why do you think people pray and come to receive my blessing? They do it so that God fulfills their wishes. Believe me, everybody wants something from God. But when God wants something from the humans, they run away. Every day they put food in front of His image, but only because they know that He does not come and eat it. If He had been coming, they would put down nothing.

People nowadays think that they are smarter than God. Let me tell a story. There was once a father whose right arm was suddenly paralyzed. In his desperation, he started to pray to God with full passion. God then appeared. He promised God to donate a hundred thousand rupees to the local temple if he could be freed of the paralysis. God had compassion and healed him. However, as soon as the man could move his arm freely, he forgot what he had promised God.

One day his wife reminded him: "God had mercy on you. He healed your arm and you do not want to keep your promise. That is not right!" Her husband said, "Be quiet!! I never said when I would donate the money. He should wait!" God listened to his words and paralyzed his arm immediately. The man became angry and called: "O God, why did you do that?" God replied: " I did not tell you how long I would heal your paralysis." We should not try to outsmart God. Use your intelligence to fulfill your daily needs and to earn your living; that is enough. God does not want your intelligence. He wants your love.

Sri Balasai Baba _____

God is responding

F

FAITH

Devotee*: If God lives in each human being, why is it so hard to have faith?*

BABA: Because you do not always know that God lives within you. God is always in you, but if you are not aware of His presence, how can He contact you? Once you feel attracted to Him, He can become active in your heart and help you. All that separates you from God is only your ignorance!

Trust in God is more important than anything else. Put your life at the feet of God, think of Him, believe in Him and dedicate to Him your thoughts, words and deeds. Then you can be absolutely sure that He is always here for you. Should it happen that you have to leave your body and die, God will be present at the moment of your death. He will take you to Him. Then you are either united with Him or you have to come back on the planet earth to be reborn in another form. In any case one thing is for sure: If you think of Him during your life, then it will be His prime task to take care of you, in this life and the next.

The sole difficulty you have to overcome is to get me, to catch me and to win me for yourself. Once you have completely opened your heart, I will never leave you. Even if you do not think of me any more, I will be with you. **There is no more important exercise for you than thinking of me as often as possible.**

FOOD

Devotee: What about food?

BABA: Eating fish breeds negative qualities, like wrath, greed, brutality, jealousy, envy, etc. The energy of the meat gives you negative impulses. If you eat a vegetarian diet, you will get positive power. The biggest and strongest animals, like buffalos or elephants, eat green food, fruits and vegetables. They live to be very old.

Eating a lot of potatoes makes you thick. It is also not good for the joints. If you prefer hot drinks like tea or coffee, you should have a maximum of three small cups during the day; more will be harmful. If you drink more than three small cups, you will fill up your entire belly. That is not good.

You always have to eat enough to maintain a good energy level. With each meal you should eat a little bit of dal vegetables, since dal is full of vitamins and protein.

If you eat with your hands, then use your palms and not only the finger. To eat with the fingertips is fashionable, but no energy flows into the food.

Devotee: Why do we have to learn to share?

BABA: If we eat something in front of other people, we have to share it with them. If we do not, we generate bad karma, since we are stirring up the desires of others. If we do not want to share, then we must eat by ourselves, when no one is watching.

God is responding

You should always buy enough food to share with others. We have to share each fruit with our brothers and sisters. You know our food is very rich, diverse and nutritious. You always have good rice, a wide variety of vegetables, sauces and ghee, yogurt and buttermilk. There are so many poor people. Every day they eat only cheap rice and a little bit of vegetables. They must perform hard labor with only that miserable meal in their bellies. **Therefore, you should be very grateful to the Lord for the marvelous nourishment that He has bestowed upon you. Through His grace alone do you get your daily food.**

Devotee: Baba shares always with us.

BABA: There is a reason for that. But this law does not only apply to food. There are people who will desire your clothing, your jewelry, your TV, or your stereo. Of course you do not have to give away these items, even if they call you stingy and withdraw their affection from you. **Love should not be bought with presents.**

Devotee: Many spiritual teachers do not want that their disciples to eat onions or garlic?

BABA: Yes, they do tell their disciples what to eat. For beginners it is good. But we should not forget that in reality, the purity of the mind and of the heart matters the most. Shirdi Sai Baba loved to eat onions and garlic. On a beautiful day, two men passed him and saw him eating onions and garlic. They said nasty things about him. They wondered how he could call himself a Yogi, since he ate the onions and garlic that promote the daze in humans. Shirdi called them to ask what they were saying about him. They replied, "You look like a Yogi but you eat things that are commonly known to promote the daze." Unequivocally he said: "It is the mind that covers the spiritual world with darkness, not the onions or the garlic. Those who possess the power of control can eat what they want."

FREE WILL

Devotee: If this universe is a game of God, if He is the boss we are His marionettes, then how can we influence our lives? Is there something like free will?

BABA: Whether you like it or not, whether you accept it or not, God is the author of your life story. If you think that you have a free will, then you should know that this free will was given by God. Whether you are stupid or intelligent, rich or poor, black or white, it is God who decides what you are and what you shall have.

For the spiritually inclined person, there is no free will, for they have completely dedicated themselves to God. For them, only divine will exists. People with a materialistic attitude assume that they possess free will. But things only happen through divine power. Not even a leaf on a tree will move without God's will.
Where is this so-called free will? Everything happens through karma. God is karma. He is the only actor. You only have enough free will to determine what is good and what is bad. But to put your decision into action requires divine power. Whether you walk, talk, or act - it is always God who walks, speaks and acts through you. Everything is in God's hands.

G

GIFTS

Devotee*: Some people object to the fact that Baba presents people with material items. They think that he should only give mental or spiritual gifts.*

BABA: Baba asks people what they want. A lot of people seek material things. You should be happy with what you have. But I am really here to bring you on the right path and to accompany you on that path. When you have gathered enough experience in the material world, when you know in your heart that there you can only find temporary pleasures, then someday you will come to the spiritual path and search for God.

GOALS

Devotee*: How can we stay focused on our goal?*

BABA: If we know our goal then we should not care what others say. We should not become a victim of their attempt to get us to stray from our goal. It requires a certain stubbornness to finish something that you have decided to start. For this good kind of stubbornness I bless you.
There is only one worthy goal in the life of a human: to walk with God and to become one with God.

Devotee: *In the West, we believe that the meaning of life is to relish it completely.*

BABA: You can enjoy everything, but you should never forget God. Your life will be meaningless without God.

Devotee: *How can I develop mentally?*

BABA: A person who wants to develop mentally should focus on an ideal, a goal. He should live and work for that goal. He should neither think about himself, nor about what other people think! **He should also forget about liberation and concentrate exclusively on his spiritual practices. Upon such humans God will pour his blessings.**

Devotee: *Baba, how can I think of becoming one with God when I presently have no goal in my life?*

BABA: If you are without any goal, then you can decide to remember the names of God. Tell yourself: "I will never forsake Him." God will be happy about your decision and He will take care of you.

Devotee: *If it is my life goal to make a pilgrimage to Mecca, then may I not also visit my girlfriend along the way?*

BABA: You need to have a goal for which you live. On your way to that goal, you should walk straight forward without distraction. Live in society, but do not get attached to it. Be like a white bug living in the muck heap. Though he lives in the muck heap, the bug never loses his white dress. Though you live in the swamp of society, do not get spoiled by it. The name of God on your lips will serve as your life raft. He will keep you afloat.

GOD

Devotee: What is God?

BABA: We can never say how God really is. He does not possess this or that characteristic. He is a reflection of those who address Him. He will show the friendly one friendliness, He will show the wrathful one wrath and He will show the jealous one jealousy. God is like a mirror. He does not have an identity. God is everything.

We could talk forever about God. This topic is inexhaustible. God does not have a true form. He is and stays indescribable. God is like a gigantic ocean. You human beings can never truly grasp His complete greatness. If you go to the ocean and draw a cup of ocean water, how much water fits into the cup? Just as the ocean's size is immeasurable, you cannot comprehend God's totality. Even if you read two thousand books about Him, He remains incomprehensible and indescribable.

You cannot understand God with your mind alone. God is as deep and unfathomable as the ocean depths. To read good books is a useful way to pass the time, but it does not bring you any closer to God. A lot of people have spent their entire life asking a lot of philosophical questions, only to finally discover that everything is a mystery and remains a mystery.

I will tell you a secret: The more you ask, the more you need to suffer. The truths I teach are self-sufficient, but you have to be inwardly stable to listen to them. Be happy and make others happy. That is enough.

Sri Balasai Baba

Devotee: *How can I get to know more about God?*

BABA: Try to explore Him, to look for Him, to experience more and more of Him. Ask yourself: Who is He? – How is He? And where is He? By exploring in this manner, you will forget yourself. That is good.

God can best be reached with a pure heart, full of love. Nothing else is necessary. God does not need to speak to you personally. His words and teachings can be experienced in everything and through everything.

Gods' messengers can reach you in various ways, by dreams or experience, for example. God has a lot of ways to teach you. Think about God and love Him; He will be your servant. He does not need material things. There is no need for any practices. You cannot directly reach God only through such practices as pranayama *(breathing exercises)*, yoga, meditation and the like. God cannot be reached physically.

But at the same time, you cannot simply think about God 24 hours a day. Simply sitting around without direction is not good. Some physical practices might help to focus your mind on God.

If you converse with others, be aware that you only talk about God and divine issues. Pray to God before you start your work and dedicate your work to Him. Then do your duty. Eventually, you will be free from karma. It is important that you do everything with devotion and a full heart. A true devotee is always completely focused on God. If such a devotee forgets God for a few minutes, then sorrow and pain will overcome him as if his dearest son was about to die.
But you have to make the effort and start walking in God's way. God

is love; love is God. He knows exactly what his protégé needs to advance, just as the mother knows exactly what her child needs. Only she knows when it needs something to eat, when it has eaten enough, when it needs to be bathed, etc. The child gives himself up to the care of its mother. If it has a desire, then it does not stop demanding until that desire is fulfilled. So should it be with you and God, but you should beg for liberation from the eternal circle of life and death. One day you will be liberated and become one with me!

You may have read a lot of books and acquired a lot of knowledge. Here we want only to practice implementing these ideas. If I want to do something good for the world, does this happen through mere thoughts? No! Only if we put our good thoughts into actions are they useful. Only then can something marvelous happen. If you only remember one thing that I have said, remember this: Practice, practice and transfer. To melt sugar in one's mouth is better than asking somebody how the sugar tastes. Eat for me, work for me, sing for me and meditate for me, do everything for me – then you will be able to know God.

In this world, nothing is permanent but the love of God. Therefore, you should give up all relationships with transient things and open yourself up to God's love. God's love is true love. You bind yourself throughout your entire life to a woman, to children, to friends and to innumerable objects, but only God is eternal.

If you do not give God one minute of attention, what will you do when you face death and God takes you into the other world? Your family members can only accompany you to your incineration or your funeral.

Sri Balasai Baba

God will guide you and be at your side, but you have to integrate Him into your life and be fully available to Him. Otherwise your body is like a leather bag, simply collecting nutrition, sleeping and procreating. That is the life of an animal. Use this unique opportunity to lead a divine life. Live the spiritual values of truth and practice the right behavior: peace, pure love and non-violence. Only then can you call yourself a human.

Devotee: *Is God only love?*

BABA: If God had been incessantly punishing people and beating people up, as many people imagine, His hands would have been swollen and His stick would have been broken into pieces. How can you believe in a beating and punishing God? Do you think He likes to punish?

But neither does God jump down from heaven in order to distribute gifts. **God's love and blessings are always present.** His gifts are always there. **I want to take the fear of God away from society. God is pure love, pure compassion, pure friendliness, pure grace and pure blessing.**

Devotee: *Are people still afraid of God at all?*

BABA: Nowadays the people are very ignorant and they do not have any respect for God anymore. They think that there is no God who sees and knows everything.

I want to tell a little story from the Koran. There was once a young woman whose mother suddenly became very sick. She had to be treated with a certain medicine. She met a rich man in the street and she decided to ask, "Please give me a little bit of money. My mother is

God is responding

very sick and she urgently needs medicine. We are very poor and we cannot buy anything."
The man offered her a kind of exchange: I will give you money, but first I want to amuse myself with you." When she heard that, she turned to her God and begged him: "I will give away my body and I am also ready to die, but please preserve the life of my mother, who brought me to this earth and sacrificed so much for my sake."

She went to the man's room. When she arrived, he demanded that she close all the doors and windows. He told her to cover even the smallest cracks so that no light could enter the room. She carried out all his orders, but when she was done she said, "Now that I have done as you asked, it is very dark in this room. But you can never close the eyes of my God, who will hear and watch everything."

He was not expecting such a remark. He became very uncertain. He was even afraid and he was not able to do what he had wanted to. He gave her the money and disappeared. Like this young lady who had a deep personal relationship with God, you should be aware that He sees and knows everything. **See only God with your eyes. Let your hands act only for God and good things.**

Life is very fragile, like a soap bubble that can burst at any moment. Throughout your entire life, you have probably had your mind on money, sex, property, husband, wife, children and amusements. What a tremendous waste!!! One day you will have to die and leave this world. Who will then take care of you? Your relatives will honor you at the cemetery. But from there, only God can lead you to other worlds. He will see all your past deeds. He will decide whether to lead you further or not. Some take their own lives away before it is their time. God is the only one who can give life or take it away. If you end life before the end of your natural lifespan, then you will have to suffer.

Devotee: *Please tell me: Where is God? In me? Behind me?*

BABA: Wherever you are, He is there too. If you think of Him or if you pray to Him, then He will be with you. If you image that God is in your mind, then God will be with you.

Devotee: *Are we a part of God?*

BABA: You are not only part of God; you are God! In India we say: "Aham Brahma Asmi", which means: I am myself the Brahman, the Absolute, the Spirit. Imagine a dead and a living body. The living body possesses something that the dead body lacks. This is the spirit-Brahman. As soon as Brahman is present in the body, it blindfolds the body and the human thinks that it is the body only. How Brahman acts in each creature depends upon that creature's karma. One day each of you will perceive and experience that he is Brahman and that he always has been Brahman.

It was Shankara who first taught humans that there is no difference between God and themselves. In the universe there exists only this one God, no other. This teaching we call Advaita – the unity of all existence. The great Shankara had the ability to see God and communicate with Him in all His forms. God can take on any form, but His true essence is formless.

God lives in all beings and He loves them all. In His love there is no separation. God loves every creature, even the leper and the ugly ones. But the human being loves only that which he likes. God does not observe a human being with His eyes. **He looks into the heart of His creature.** The relationship between God and those who love Him is a relationship of spirit.

Devotee: How can I experience a state where I am one with God?

BABA: This is a good question. You are a student of philosophy; you have read and heard a lot about religions and leaders of different religions. However, this is not enough to merge with God. You need a deeper spiritual understanding of the things that you already know intellectually. If you concentrate on the name and form of God, you will always remember Him. Thereby you forget yourself; God will come one day and give you everything.

I do not say that you should believe in me or pray to me - this up to you. First of all, you should find a means by which you want to become one with God. Before you can harvest a fruit, you have to plant a tree, cherish it and let it grow. This requires a lot of time and patience. You have to wait till the fruit ripens. Whatever happens, accept it.

Devotee: In my opinion, I can only merge with a formless God. Will I be caught in the illusory world if I venerate God in the form of a human?

BABA: No. If you look for happiness in your sweetheart, then you will certainly fall into the clutches of illusion. Here we must differentiate. You will not fall into illusion if you venerate a divine incarnation. This you cannot call illusion. The true danger lies in getting involved with fatal entanglements in the material world.

Devotee: Moses received the Ten Commandments from God. One commandment is as follows: You should not make yourself an image of God.

BABA: That time has passed. We now live in the 21st century. You should concentrate on what happens now, not on what had happened thousands of years ago. The days of Moses are over. **Through the form you reach the formless.** The direct way to God, through formlessness, is very difficult.

Sri Rama reincarnated to permeate his society with righteousness and truth. When Sri Krishna came, he brought love and peace. My message and duty is to strengthen humanity among the people on this earth. Nowadays the people on this earth are full of envy, anger, pride and hatred. There is a lack of concentration and dedication to the divine, the eternal. Therefore, I give you the only commandment: Think of God! In any way you can, you should love God.

Devotee: *In India, one encounters a lot of gods. How many gods are there?*

BABA: Take your father as an example. He is a single person, but he is the son of his mother, the father of his children, the husband of his wife and the brother of his sisters.

The same applies to God. He is called by many names, but there is only one God. You call me Allah, Jesus, Bhagavan, Rama or Rahim. Each call, each emotion that comes from you reaches me. Behind the diversity of names one finds unity. There are many paths to God, but the goal is always the same. God's presence cannot be limited to a single and definite location. God is everywhere. God is everything.

God does not have a form. He is like a gold bar. You can take that gold bar and make your own jewelry, in whatever shape you please. Therefore choose the form that suits you best. If you think, 'God is my son or father or mother or master,' then the relationship with Him will be quite different than between you and an abstract God. This is the simple and joyful way to Him.

If a human has a strong desire to become one with God, it will happen. But everything ultimately depends on the will of God. However, when one's aspiration for union with God is very great, merging with God can come more easily.

Devotee: *And if we pass everything on to God?*

BABA: If we pass our problems on to God, God will take full responsibility for them. Humans think that God does not have any problems, but all the problems of all humanity belong to Him.

Try to understand that the entire universe is in the hand of God. You are only the marionettes in His game; God operates through you. Meditate on this truth always. Then you can easily accept any situation that you may face in your life.

If you do this, then you are not going to identify yourself with happiness or sorrow, for everything belongs to God, not to you. Joy and affliction belong together like day and night, heat and coldness, light and darkness. Learn to be indifferent to both happiness and affliction. If you have managed that, your life will be simple, joyful and full of happiness, you will actively see the will of God wherever you look. Only then will there be peace in you. Only then will you be truly happy.

In order to be successful in the external world, you have to make a lot of effort. You waste a lot of time and energy, for nothing. If you work spiritually for God, you will also become tired. But it is very good to become tired while working for God. Thereby you will obtain his blessings and become liberated. It is crucial to be free of material thoughts, which are obstacles on the spiritual path. Every moment can be used to concentrate on God.

So do not waste your time with useless actions. **When you serve God, you make God and entire universe happy.** God is very close to you. He is your very best friend. He wants you to always be happy, for your suffering is also His suffering and your happiness is also His happiness.

In India we have so many philosophies, so many ways to go about merging with God. But there are also people who live simply with the consciousness that they came on earth to do their duty and to serve God, without being bound to anybody or anything else. Divine power does not lie in mantras, but in your trust in God.

Devotee: Is God also happy when we repeat His name mechanically?

BABA: Yes, but He is even happier when we perform it with a full heart. By constant repetition of His holy names, your heart will one day merge with Him. Mechanical repetition is acceptable at the beginning.

Devotee: What can one give to God?

BABA: What do you want to give to God? He already possesses everything. He does not need anything. But people do. We can help people in need. By serving humanity, you can serve God.

Devotee: What happens if humanity acts against God?

BABA: The wrath of God is indescribable. The snake only bites you if you want to harm it; the lion only attacks when you provoke it. And God only shows His wrath when He is unceasingly abused.

Join only the company of righteous devotees who talk positively about God. You must even leave your best friend, if he speaks badly of God. **Bad things that are said about God are not ascribed to God, but**

God is responding

to the person who says those things.

Who shall protect you if you stir up the wrath of God? If there is no escape from the wrath of a lion or a snake, how can you expect to avoid the wrath of God?

Devotee: *Baba, in what way can you stir up the wrath of God?*
BABA: When you continuously make Him angry. Like when you ask this type of question.

Devotee: *Because of that, will you condemn me?*
BABA: Never! Not this God. You do not need to be afraid! I never condemn anybody!

Devotee: *I have been looking for God my entire life, but have found nothing.*
BABA: People with good karma can approach God. But sometimes, as a result of this proximity to God, people do not recognize God, though He stands before them. They live with Him as if He were a relative, employer, etc. Those who have recognized God need to make further spiritual efforts to keep up contact with God.

You have never been away from God. This is your imagination. To show you the closeness of God, God even takes the form of a human and moves among you - as I do now. He does not sit above you, far away on a sofa, with a long thick stick in his hand. He does not beat you incessantly. God is among you and lives with you - He behaves like you. Receive God as I have recommended: with a whole heart and a happy heart.

Sri Balasai Baba

God has created a lot of fruits like bananas, apples, mangos and so on, so we should not stay hungry. Similarly, God has given us many ways to maintain contact with Him, like bhajan singing, reciting His name and other spiritual practices. Every person can choose what he prefers; he should perform this practice regularly. But all deeds must be performed in God's name. If you do not continually make the effort, you will lose contact with God. It is Baba's duty to give you what you need at the right time. It is your duty to continue making efforts.

Devotee: *Does God live in each creature?*

BABA: God is everywhere at all times. He lives in each creature. Therefore it is crucial that you learn to see God in each creature, to respect and love all things. If you make somebody suffer, then the divinity within that person will suffer. Think about this truth and act according to my words.

Devotee: *God never rests?*

BABA: God will only rest when His last child has reached liberation. Until that point, He will always return to earth to teach humans and to stand at their side. At each moment we need the help of God. We should pray that He should never forsake us.

Devotee: *On my way to God, I want to grasp any hands on the right and left side of me and pull them to Him.*

BABA: Do what you can. Be aware that you need God's energy and blessing to take people with you. Right now the energy you have is only enough for yourself. Pray to me - then I will give you more. In general, people try to get you to stray from the good path. You have to be strong so that this will not happen. Therefore I advise you: Do what you can and leave the rest up to me.

Devotee: Is it my duty to lead my grown up children onto the spiritual path, or shall I let them go their own way?

BABA: You can try to lead them, but you should not force them! If they have gathered good karma, they will decide to follow you. If not, then they won't.

The river exists to unite with the sea. Humans exist to be united with God. The ephemeral happiness that we perceive when we are with our family or when we are having sex should be the starting point to aspire for the eternal happiness. Worldly luck is only momentarily and transitory, like a sample of sweeter things. It is only a tiny part of divine happiness. Do not get stuck on material happiness. Reach for true happiness - the happiness that is eternal. Otherwise your life will be a waste.

GRACE

Devotee: Baba, in the New Testament we learn that union with God cannot be attained by our own efforts, but only by His grace.

BABA: Do you want to know now if this is true or not?

Devotee: No, I want to know if it means that our spiritual efforts are purposeless.

BABA: No, not at all! Why do you perform spiritual rituals? You practice them to please God and to make Him happy. God is pleased by your practice and pours His grace over you. Therefore, always try to please God. That is how to win His heart. He gives you what you need - that is His grace! Therefore do not think: "I do this or that to advance on my path." Think: "Whatever I do, it is for God, for His pleasure."

Why did God come down to this earth in a human form? I came to create good relationships between people. I want to unite the humans and lead them to a divine unity. This is the reason I came. When we hurt others, then we will punish ourselves through the actions that come back to us. It then looks like God is punishing us. If children are naughty and do bad things, then the mother will punish them, in order to improve them and bring them on the right track. She only does this because she loves the children. You are all my children - children of God. Not just you, but all creatures in the universe are my children. If you show love and affection to God and all creatures in the universe, then you will also experience only love and affection. Do not be afraid, but have love and affection for God.

Devotee: It was your divine grace that gave me healing.

BABA: Without divine grace there is no healing and without efforts there is no grace; both are necessary. **Therefore, do your best. God does the rest!**

If a devotee loves me very much, if he renders me absolute confidence and great devotion, then I will shower him with grace.

Devotee: Could faith heal me?

BABA: Look at God's grace. This devotee does not touch me, talk to me, or expect anything from me. Her faith in God has healed her. **A lot of people try to direct my attention towards them by giving**

money or doing something physically, but this is not the right way. To receive something from God one needs unshakable faith and the grace of God.

Do not forget that you must make spiritual efforts! Many people come here because they want to get rings or chains from me. They bring a lot of problems that they want me to solve for them. Within a second they want to be liberated from old age and chronic suffering. Is this possible? I might be able to heal them, but what about their contributions? They should cooperate! If I do not produce a spontaneous healing, then they drive home and complain that Baba did not do anything for! **But where is their contribution?**

Devotee: Baba, when you heal the sick ones, do you abrogate the laws of nature?

BABA: I do not want to annul the laws of nature. I will only do it if it is absolutely necessary. But people must be patient. Humans who have been suffering for 30 years come here and expect immediate healing. I tell them that I can heal half of the disease; the rest is up to them.

GREED

BABA: Greedy people cannot reach God. They are not willing to give in order to receive again. They do not have any friends, because whenever anybody approaches them in a friendly manner, they panic, thinking that this person might want something from them. They always think, "When he comes to me, what he will then bring? When I come to him, what will I get?"

GURU – SPIRITUAL MASTER

Devotee: What is the difference between a guru and a divine incarnation?

BABA: The guru teaches you spiritual practices and shows you the way to God. But a divine incarnation is God Incarnate – there is nothing to show. The guru may teach you how to awaken the divine within you. God gives you wisdom through His grace. The guru has disciples. God has devotees. The guru can give you wisdom, but he himself gets his own wisdom from God. An enlightened person seeks only to merge with God.

Here, at the ashram, you have the extraordinary luck of having God as your master. **Listen to me when I am teaching and treat me as your guru. In the times of meditation, however, focus on me as your God. Here you can listen to the words of God as you see Him in front of you. In this ashram, it is possible to see God before you, even as you discover Him within yourself. Here God is visible and present on all levels.

There are people who sit in full view of a divine incarnation, but still they seek to go through a jungle or into a dark cave to find God. They yearn to go from light to darkness, because they do not perceive that God is in front of them. **There is no difference between an embodied God and the bodiless light. Whether you venerate God as an embodied spirit or as a formless being, the result is the same.**

Here are some of the differences between a divine incarnation and self-made enlightened person, sage, guru, prophet, or priest:

1. I do what they only talk about.
2. They are not always capable of practicing what they preach.
3. I cause what I say and I talk about that which I cause.
4. I teach, I bless and I help. The priest talks about chastity, but one of them might rape children and have homosexual relationships with young boys.

Nowadays many so-called wise gurus become angry about insignificant things, curse, blame others for problems, or act sadistically. The West is full of such people. They do not know about God or divinity. They only talk about their own imaginations; they lead people astray. In this manner they commit a great sin for which they will one day have to pay. By their sinful behavior they create their own dreadful suffering.

The so-called prophets talk about non-violence, but they kill in the name of God to force people to accept their self-made religious opinions.

Sri Balasai Baba

There are many gurus and a lot of people follow them. These adherents are normally called disciples. If a disciple meets a guru, then he might serve him his entire life without getting anything. If the guru is old, then the disciple has to take care of him. There are many people who give the guru everything they possess and serve him unselfishly, without having gotten anything that would have advanced them on the spiritual level. A guru can merely show his disciples the way to God. He is a mediator between the disciple and God.

The guru cannot do anything himself. The guru has certain skills, like reading thoughts or materializing objects. He has obtained those skills by way of spiritual practice. But just as God has given him these abilities and God can take them away again.
A divine incarnation has no disciples, only devotees. A guru possesses only limited powers; a divine incarnation possesses all powers. The divine incarnation is omnipresent, omniscient and almighty. A divine incarnation can at any moment lift the devotee into a higher consciousness or convey any perception. For that, the physical presence of the devotee is not necessary.

A divine incarnation can influence anything at all and change everything without any physical contact with what he is changing. A divine incarnation can protect and assist you, no matter where you are. A devotee can be anywhere - he needs only think of the divine incarnation and God will be present. Since God is in everything, there is no place where God does not exist! It is direct contact with God!

A guru, on the other hand, requires the physical presence of his disciple to convey knowledge. The disciple depends on the physical presence of the guru in order to get something from him. Why do you

God is responding

need a detour via a guru? If you ask the guru for something, then he will pray to God for it. Here you do not need a mediator. You can directly convey your wishes to God.

Devotee: *Please bless me on all levels.*

BABA: I bless you on all levels, but you have to think of me. When you go back to your home country, always think of me. Only then will my blessings be effective.

Devotee: *How do I know that the master that I meet is truly my master?*

BABA: You can only pray. Your karma will determine your destiny. On the credit side of your spiritual account, there are good merits from your former life. Only because of that are you able to pray. Time and circumstance will regulate everything.

To find a guru is not that easy. To verify if a guru is a true or spurious one is even more difficult. In your heart you will know if you have found a guru. From the first moment you see him, your heart will be filled with affection and love for him. Your hands will come together for the holy greeting and you will want to bow down in front of him. The way he acts will tell you everything. Your heart will tell you if he is the right master for you.

A master can guide you quickly to your goal, but first you have to find one you can trust and accept. The master will spark the divine light in you and guide you, if you let him. However, following a master is not always very comfortable. Weaknesses and fears - previously buried deep within your mind - will be transmitted to the surface of your consciousness. The master presents you with yourself; he shows you your own reflection and destroys your limited little ego. In order to enable you to grow, he gives you tests and puts obstacles in your way. Welcome these gifts, for they are going to help you.

Sometimes there are materializations and so-called miracles. These exist in order to spiritually awaken you. Although they seem superficial, beneath them lies a great and precious treasure. Do not be satisfied until you get the treasure. Once you have started on the spiritual path, you should never stand still. Continue walking. You need to be patient. It may take numerous lives to achieve your goal, but stick to it. Reading and talking about God is not sufficient to experience oneness with Him. A seed in the earth needs good soil, water and sun to grow. It is the same with humans. They cannot attain their goal immediately; it takes time and above all patience.

Devotee: *Does one have to decide which master to follow? Should one go back and forth between masters?*

BABA: **If you do not decide, you will remain a seeker for the rest of your life.** It is like a superficial romantic relationship. If a lover thinks that someone else might be better, they will go to that person and never be content with what they have. In spiritual life it is similar. **I want you to decide and stick with your decision, because only then will a deep experience be possible with the master.** There are always humans who will try to distract you from the way. This is quite normal. You have to be firm in what you have decided.

It is better to die then to leave your master to search for a new one. It is like a treasure hunt. It is better to dig in one spot than in many. An intelligent person will do whatever he can to recover the entire treasure, rather than being satisfied with minor precious things here and there.

God is responding

A guru is like the flashlight that you need to find your way through the darkness. At the end of your journey you will reach the true light. You should stay with one guru, even if he is not completely enlightened. The power of God will work through him. The light of his flashlight might not be that bright, but God will act through your master. He will give you what you need.

I repeat: One guru is sufficient. If you have decided to stay with him, then you should try to get his blessings by trying to learn something from him. You must be worthy of his holy knowledge.

Try to put his words into practice, for spirituality has nothing to do with theoretical knowledge. We could sit together many days and talk about one topic after another. But will change it you? – Not at all. Be awake for what your guru says – you will get his blessings by trying to be like him, by giving him your love and by trying to put his teachings into practice. A true guru will love his disciple as if he were the guru's only child; he will try to bring him on the right path.

Try to love your master and show him love, devotion and trust. If you win the love of the master, then he will shower you with his blessings. Be patient. In due time Baba will satisfy all your wishes.

Devotee: *Are you quite strict as a master?*

BABA: A master who takes his responsibilities seriously will be strict. To teach effectively, sometimes he has to become quite furious. This anger does not last very long. It appears within a part of a second and shows itself only outwardly. Inwardly I am completely calm. My heart melts for the other person. In the worst cases I might not speak to the person for years. Sometimes it is necessary to teach.

I am not the kind of master who does not allow his disciples to approach him. We do not have to create an artificial distance to guarantee respect between the master and his disciple. If I am not close to all of you, I am unhappy.

HAPPINESS

Devotee: Baba, your eyes are not like ours. They are shining with happiness. What do we have to do to make our eyes radiate?

BABA: These rays of happiness come from the heart. Whatever we do, we must do it with a full heart. We must forget ourselves. Only then will we feel deep contentment and joy in our hearts. Happiness appears only if you act with full devotion and attention.

Devotee: How can I be happy?

BABA: Everybody in the universe wants peace and happiness. **Happiness stems from being content with what you have. Contentment is the absence of wishes, the lack of expectation of how something must be.** Once you can accept any life situation, without always seeking to change it, you are at peace and you feel happy. If you love God, then everything will be very easy and simple. You know that everything comes from God and everything goes back to God. Then you accept everything that comes as a gift from God. Accept the bad as a sacrifice to God. Be grateful for the good things.

Observe all your thoughts, deeds and words. Before you act, ask yourself whether what you want to do is good and useful or not. Thereby you train your discrimination. You might have a lot of emotions, feelings and inclinations. When they emerge, observe them.

Sri Balasai Baba

Perceive them, but do not follow them if they are not useful or good. You might be willing to sacrifice good things for an object you desire. Once you possess that which you desire, it loses it value to you. Then the next great desire arises in you. The happiness that you can find in this world is not permanent. But the happiness that you can find through union with God is the greatest possible happiness.

It is easy to be happy and joyful when everything works out well. It is also easy to see why people get sad when something does not work out. We can only be happy and joyful if we can see the good in everything and are able to laugh about it. How can we do that? First we need to decide that we need to be happy. We must get rid of the things we depend upon. If we expect that somebody outside ourselves must do something good for us to be satisfied, then we will be hopelessly lost. So we practice every day to try to find the good, even in bad situations. We must look for a reason to be happy.

How often you sleep with each other, until it becomes boring? Or if you like watching TV, after three hours your eyes grow tired and you want to switch off the TV. Or if you listen to music, how long can you do that before you get bored? All the joy of this world comes and goes; it does not last. You can experience that every day. But there is happiness beyond this world that is everlasting and never-ending. The joy you perceive while performing spiritual exercises is the key to it.

The sweetest thing in life is never-ending divine bliss. The happiness that you find in the relationships between humans lasts only briefly. It is only temporary.

By being always sad we destroy ourselves. My duty is to bless you! Your duty is to control your desires; only wish for things that will positively enrich your life. Be happy so that your sadness will not spread to others. Being happy, even when there is no reason for it, requires great spiritual composure. It is an exercise worth practicing. Nothing in the world is permanent; we are only guest performers on the stage of life.

Devotee: *Should a depressed person meditate?*

BABA: Depression is a terrible social malady. **Meditation is a general medicine** and those who meditate will be liberated from their depression. If someone seeks liberation, he must first learn to balance his wayward mind. He may not wander between extreme pleasures and extreme sadness.

Everything that happens is for the best. God loves you more than a thousand mothers; He always wants what is best for you. **Every time God sees your needs and fulfills them, you can be sure that they were good wishes. Whenever He does not fulfill your wishes, then you can be certain that the fulfillment of those wishes would not have been for your benefit.**

Devotee: *Do you have to leave your family to be happy?*

BABA: I say: "Be happy!" I do not say: "Renounce and suffer for God!" as the old prophets said. I do not demand that you leave your family and go into the jungle in order to reach God. I allow you to enjoy everything life has to offer - but do not forsake God. If you do your best on the material and spiritual levels, if you fulfill your duties instead of running away from them, then you will find total liberation. If you conscientiously fulfill your duties on the material level without looking at the benefits you derive from them, if you leave everything to God, then your karmic cycle will end and liberation will automatically occur. You will have reached God.

The divine teachers, gurus and prophets can teach you, but you have to put their words into practice yourself. If you live by divine words, then God is ready to give you His blessings. To listen is not enough. Do your best and fulfill your duties mindfully, but leave the results to God.

Your duty is to venerate God and to serve Him. God knows what He has to give you. You do not have to give up ephemeral happiness, but try to aspire for eternal happiness. Do not forget God, even as you enjoy worldly happiness. The former prophets and divine teachers preached that you have to suffer for God. I tell you that you can reach me happily. Love and humanity will lead you to God. God is happiness; therefore He wants His children to be happy. It is not God's desire to see you with sad faces.

Devotee: *How does laughing affect our body?*
BABA: Laughing is healthy - it relaxes our body and mind.

Devotee: *For fourteen years I have spent most of my time in India. Why do I only meet you now?*
BABA: This is the right moment for you to experience all kinds of happiness. Being happy yourself is the only way to make others happy.

I bless you with the words: Be happy. That means, "do not worry." I am always there for you. You do not need to ask me for anything in particular, because through my blessing, everything will come to you at the right moment.

When I talk about happiness or joy, I do not mean it in a traditional sense. Being happy means that whatever happens, you won't be out of balance. Even if sad things approach us, we simply let them happen. We are happy, knowing that everything in the divine comedy happens for a reason. Try always to be happy. Thereby you will please God. God is always happy. God is happiness- and happiness is God.

HEALING

Devotee: A physician gives patients various medicines and therapies, but sometimes they do not work…

BABA: The physician can only treat the body of the patient. **He has no insight into the heart of the patient; he does not see the karmic steps the patient has taken.** The physician needs to know that he is only a mediator between God and the patient. His attitude should be: 'I treat the patient. God heals the patient.' If the patient has good karma, then the medicine helps and the person gets healed. **Sometimes our karma will not permit us to heal.** The physician has to give his best and his duty, but he must put the fate of his patients in God's hands.

The prime duty of a physician is to encourage a patient to continue living. **He is not allowed to take away the patient's courage to live and he may not stop consoling the patient. Until the patient's last breath, the physician has to make him believe that everything will turn out well.** Consoling, encouraging and creating confidence are very important. How often has a dangerously ill person experienced healing at the last second and stood up from bed miraculously healed? If the physician includes God in his work and the patient possesses faith in God, God will bless both physician and patient.

(Baba speaks from the point of view of the patient:) A sick spiritual seeker should undergo medical treatment and **never stop believing that God will heal him.** Hence, I send you to the physician if something is wrong with you! **You must trust in his abilities and consolations. You should not wait around passively for the sickness to disappear.**

Devotee: What is Laya Yoga?

BABA: Let's say that you have a tumor on your arm. The practice of Laya Yoga can melt it away. Concentrate on the sick spot and mentally recite the Sanskrit sounds that correspond to that part of the body. That can heal your tumor. Using the Sanskrit sounds to concentrate solely on God generates tremendous divine powers. This ancient technique is divine knowledge. Laya Yoga can heal, but its true objective is to give us a way to unify with God. Its healing powers are only incidental to that goal.

HEART

Devotee: How will I know if I am on a good path?

BABA: Your inner heart - your intuition - will guide you. If your husband tells you, "Darling, everything I do is only to make you happy!" then your inner heart will tell you immediately if this is the truth. It is the same here. To find out if you are on the right track, to discover whether your alignment is good, you need only to listen to your inner heart!

Devotee: Does God make any distinction between a male and a female heart?

BABA: From the point of view of God, there is no difference between man and woman. He is not interested in the body. He looks only at the quality of the heart.

Devotee: Baba, you say that you come when we present you food and that you leave if we forget you afterwards. But where do you go? Don't you also say that you live in our heart?

BABA: Are you truly aware that Baba lives in your heart? If you are aware that He is your engine, then you do not need to put down anything in front of His picture. But you need to believe wholeheartedly.

Devotee: How can we learn to hear God's voice in our hearts?

BABA: You are like a radio receiver that has to tune into the right station before it can receive anything. Learn to concentrate on your inner heart; it will convey to your brain what is right for you.

Devotee: Baba, how can we become pure hearts?

BABA: **You have to learn to love everybody and to see Baba in every creature. This exercise demands a lot of patience.** Therefore, begin today, so that you may someday become a master in this discipline. If people tease you because of your devotion, stay indifferent and try to feel love for them. If you can do this you will have reached the highest level of purity.

Remember that the body is only an instrument; it is ephemeral. You have to learn to be detached from it. Every moment, you must be prepared to die.

One day I closed my eyes beneath a tree in the ashram. A few boys came and urinated over my shoulder. I did react and as a result, they left. Another time I was attacked by scorpions on that same spot. But when I opened my eyes, they all lay dead. My energy had killed them.

You have to be forever ready to say farewell to this world. The body does not exist forever. If you truly love God, you should be willing to die. Men are going to scold and criticize you. They might betray you, as Jesus was betrayed by his disciple. **If you truly love God, do not worry about the blame and praise of others**. Be indifferent and do not suffer if others want to harm you. Do not stop loving God, whatever happens. **He will test your faith and your love.** Negativity will try to come and seduce you. You have to face these tests.

Devotee: *Does God only see a pure heart?*

BABA: God sees all hearts. If all hearts had been pure already, why would He have come to earth? Only by transforming an impure heart into a pure one does He show His true greatness.

Devotee: *How can I present you my heart?*

BABA: Each human being possesses a body, a mind and a heart. The mind rules over the body, but the heart should control the mind. Although karma may dictate our circumstances on earth, we can still use our minds and hearts to do good. Integrate God into your thoughts and feelings and you will have the control over yourself. He leads you on the right path and in the course of time you will perceive that all actions originate from God. Do not exclude Him from any area of your life.

Every day you can use your mind to tell your heart to go to Baba! Thoughts, words and deeds should always match. **Our words should always whole-heartedly match our actions.** Once we put everything in the hands of God, he takes over responsibility for good and for evil.

We need our entire essence to find God. In former times, the orthodox Brahmin prayed: "Lord, let me be your instrument. Take my hands to present the rites of sacrifices, my eyes to see you everywhere and my mouth that I always repeat your name and talk about you. All parts of body should only serve you. Lead me onto the right path."

HEAVEN

Devotee: *Baba, what lies beyond heaven?*

BABA: Beyond heaven lies God alone. Do not seek heaven. Yearn for God. You will reach heaven if you have done good deeds in your life. Only if you reach unity with God, there will be no more rebirths, no more reincarnations. You will be forever free.

Sri Balasai Baba

HOLIDAYS

Devotee: *How should we handle holidays?*

BABA: People don't understand the meaning and purpose behind holidays any more. They spend the day eating, drinking and sleeping a lot. They think that this is an adequate way to spend the day. This is a big mistake. A holiday should be lived in memory of a great saint who came to earth and sacrificed his life for all of humanity. Christ spilled his blood for all humanity; he suffered tremendously. Unfortunately, most people do not remember this fact. They should not call this day a holiday since they treat it as a day of feasting.

Devotee: *Today is Good Friday...*

BABA: Again, this should not be a day of feasting. It is an utterly sad day. Jesus died this morning. He sacrificed his precious life, his pure blood, for all humanity. Today you should at least remember his greatness and weep, since Jesus had to suffer so much. Always recall his selfless deeds, his teachings and his exemplary life. Try to follow him.

On such a day, one has to honor the life of saint whose name is venerated. If you only eat and sleep, then you will belittle the holiday. If you aware of God's presence all the time and you live only for Him, then every day will be a holiday.

INDIFFERENCE

Devotee: *Should we accept everything with indifference?*

BABA: Accept everything with indifference and calmness; this is enlightenment. Whatever situation you are in, stay indifferent. The so-called enlightened people of toady give speeches on enlightenment. They say, "Never become angry!" If a student then dares to ask: "O master, why aren't we allowed to become angry?" the master becomes enraged and screams: "Shut up, you idiot!" We can recognize his state of mind.

Devotee: *And if I am not in the mood?*

BABA: The human heart always seeks change. It is never satisfied and it always wants what it does not have. So one should not pay attention to moods. Once we have decided something, we should continue to pursue it, without running after new ideas and falling into one doubt after another. The heart and mind are always unsteady, inconstant. As long as we feel and think, it will be like that. Our duty is to be indifferent towards these fluctuating impulses and moods.

Sri Balasai Baba

God is responding

J

JESUS

Devotee: Yesterday, you spoke to us about Jesus. Jesus said, "I am the son of God." You said you are God. I have a problem with that. If someone in my home country says that he is God, it is unacceptable! I believe in Jesus. When you say that you are God, I have a problem with that.

BABA: Then you will always have a problem with that; nothing I can say will change your mind. This is a problem for many. It is not my duty to solve your problems for you. **Baba is at home in all religions. Each religion has its own laws.** Each will orient itself according to its own laws. Each religion has the goal of leading humans to a higher plane of spiritual existence. If you believe in Jesus, then stay with him.

The forms of God are not separated from each other. It is you who makes the separation; therefore you suffer. **Between the incarnations of God there is no power struggle and no disharmony. It is always humans who create such feelings. God is one. There is only one God.**

Two thousand years ago, Jesus said: "God is my father; I am his son. Nobody will reach my father except through me." This is my message: I am the father and the son. You can get one direct ticket to God. Jesus reached a certain level of enlightenment. Beyond all heaven there is only light, but Jesus did not speak about that.

The cross is the symbol of Christianity. It stands for our small egoistic self that needs to be crucified and killed. We should try to live for God and not for ourselves. To find Him we need to forget ourselves and love Him.

Devotee: Can I continue to pray to Jesus?

BABA: God has many forms and many names. Jesus and Baba are one! In your heart you can pray to whomever you want! **But whatever your path, you should not leave it.** All prayers are equally good! If you are happy when you direct your prayer to Jesus, then continue to do that. If you are happy while praying to Baba, then continue with that. **You can continue to represent the message of Christ, through which you reach also me.**

All religions are built on faith and trust. Their common goal is to show people the way to God. You are Christians or Muslims or Hindus because you believe in the Holy Scriptures. But all Christians are converts, are they not? Wasn't Jesus himself born a Jew? Whether you call yourself a Christian or not is unimportant. Being a true Christian is about **loving Christ in your heart and following his teachings.**

We do not want convince anybody to convert to another religion. Many so-called Christians have killed to convert people to their faith. This we do not want. Ours is the religion of love. Christ lived and taught pure love. He never ordered anyone to kill innocent humans. To be a true Christ, a person does not need to be converted to Christianity. It is sufficient that he pray to Christ from the depth of his heart, following Jesus' example of selflessness. If a person does that, then he does not need to read the Bible or to go to church, since he has a living relationship with Jesus Christ.

Christ is also Krishna. The Greek name Christos has its origin in the Sanskrit word Krsna, which later became Krishna.

Devotee: *Baba, could you please say something about Judas? What role did he play in the story of Jesus?*

BABA: He was the means by which Jesus became well known and beloved throughout the world. If Jesus had not been crucified, then he would not have been venerated for two thousand years. Every great drama needs people like Judas. Through them, God will demonstrate what it is good and what it is bad. God created a lot of characters and all of them have a role to play in His great performance.

You should understand that everything that happened in those stories was a drama, a game. At the end, the curtain fell down and everybody was in heaven. Only the atheist thinks that there is a border between heaven and hell. Those who truly love God should not believe such a thing.

Devotee: *Was the message of Jesus…love?*

BABA: Jesus Christ came to earth to fulfill his duty. Through his own example, he demonstrated how a godly life should be lived. His message - his entire life - was love. When they crucified him, he begged, "Father, forgive them, for they know not what they do." Out of ignorance, they crucified him.

Jesus was persecuted and killed because his tormentors had no character. Character is the most important thing for a human.
If you do not develop good character, you will lose everything and your life won't be worth anything any more. You need a good character to able to walk towards God, towards Jesus. Jesus gave

another message on the cross: "Examine your character and that of your children, so that they do not assume your bad qualities. Go and work on your character."

Devotee: *Tell us more about Jesus Christ.*

BABA: When Jesus went to the river Jordan, he met John the Baptist, who said that he himself was not worthy of Jesus' greatness. John had the same curly hair as Baba and wore a beard on his face. He lived in the forest, living on honey and grasshoppers. He publicly proclaimed the greatness of Christ and baptized him. At the time of his baptism, Jesus received power from God to act as a Messiah. So God sent a white dove from heaven. The dove sat down on his shoulder, giving him divine power.

Devotee: *Baba, is there a relationship between the baptism and the descent of the white dove?*

BABA: No. For Jesus it was simply time to get divine powers from God. Until that time he had worked as an carpenter for his father. He visited temples and meditated on God. He saw himself as an ambassador of God on earth and he knew that God was his real father. He publicly proclaimed it to be so. Once the powers of God had been transferred to him through the dove, his real mission as the Messiah began. Satan tried to seduce Jesus, but Jesus did not listen. Jesus was chosen because of his pure soul. He had the physical and mental power that would be necessary for his worldly duties.

Devotee: *What kind of relationship existed between Jesus and God?*

BABA: Jesus knew that he was the ambassador of God on earth. He recognized that he was the son of God. Later on, he reached the state of unity with God, saying, "My father and I are one." However, Jesus lost consciousness of this unity at the moment of his death, when he cried: "My God, my God, why have you forsaken me?"

There are many biblical passages in which Jesus prays to his father; it is obvious from these passages that there is a greater authority than Jesus himself. At night when Judas betrayed him, Jesus realized that he would die. He went up to the mountain to pray to God with his disciples. The holy man taught his disciples to pray in order to find God.

Since Christ was pure, God chose him as an instrument for His mission on earth. For the same reason, Mary was selected to be the mother of Jesus. She was a woman with a good character and lived with the continuous awareness of God's omnipresence.

Mary was a virgin when the archangel Gabriel proclaimed that she would be the mother of Jesus. She asked him how this could be, since she was not yet married. The archangel Gabriel replied that the almighty God could do anything. He told her that by the grace of God, her relative, Elisabeth, became pregnant at the age of 60. He told her that God is able to perform even greater miracles.

Sri Balasai Baba

KARMA

Devotee: *How does karma work?*

BABA: Karma simply means action. Karma is all around us. You cannot even sit down without performing some karmically significant action. To eat, to drink and to sleep is also karma. Everything that happens is based on past karma. Karma acts everywhere in the universe. It is written on your forehead. All your interests, preferences and personal tastes develop according to the karmic law.

Karma means that what you have sown is what you will harvest. You need to eat the fruits of the tree that you have planted. If you plant a coconut tree, you cannot expect a papaya. Good actions will result in good things. Bad actions result in bad things. But even if a person only has good karma, he might still have to suffer tests of his faith.

You are only able to come to this place and see me by the virtue of your good karma, the virtue of your past actions. Because you have been with me and because you had my blessings in a former life, you can now be with me in this life. In this life you reap the fruits of your former life.

You have to attain inner stability; you must be independent of everything. If you have committed your life totally to God, then you will not

Sri Balasai Baba

be touched by karma anymore. When that happens, it should be obvious that you should not intentionally do something bad. You should also not demand the fruits of your action. Every action should be devoted to God.

Karma is another way of saying that you need to accept responsibility for your actions, thoughts, reactions, attitudes and convictions. The karmic law means that you will harvest what you have sowed. That is very simple. If you want to finish your karmic cycle, then you should decide to put everything down at the lotus feet of God. Then you can be completely free and dedicate yourself to the task of being happy.

Whenever I withdraw myself from you, it means that you have aggregated bad karma that you must get rid of. I accelerate the karmic process by my behavior, because you suffer as soon as I withdraw my attention from you. Through this suffering, you accumulate merit.

Our karma is like a bank account. Your karma accumulates merit when you do good things; merit is deducted when you do bad things. However, there is one significant difference: Money can be taken away by another person. But what we have saved in our spiritual bank account can never be taken away by anybody. Our spiritual credit is the only thing we can take with us when we die. Our money must be left behind, but the blessing of God follows us wherever we go, even after we die. **Therefore we should never stop performing spiritual practices!** When we dedicate each and every breath to God, our spiritual bank balance grows.

Devotee: *There are devotees who are always in your physical vicinity.*

God is responding

BABA: The good karma that they have accumulated from previous lives enables them to sit near me. They have a positive credit balance on their karmic bank account. As soon as their credit is used up, they move away from me. That is why we have to continue to make spiritual efforts.

Devotee: The population grows from day to day. A lot of people are threatened by starvation, because there is not enough food for everybody. What do you say about that?

BABA: Here we need to speak from a spiritual point of view. Hindu mythology and philosophy teaches us that the law of karma rules the universe. What you observe and express here is nothing other than the cycle of souls. All souls are in a cycle - they come and go. **Some are promoted. Others are set back. It depends on their past actions. No new souls come to earth. Everything moves in a circle. A mosquito might be promoted, even as a bad human is degraded.**

Devotee: Where do the souls go when they die?

BABA: According to their karma, they go to different planets or different planets of existence. There are a great number of planets. Karma determines where the soul goes; the circumstances of our rebirth depend upon our past karma, good or bad. If someone brings along a bundle of good karma as a result of the good karma he accumulated in his previous life, then he will be reborn as a human. If he doesn't use his life for positive ends, he regresses to an earlier state and he must suffer again. He will be reborn as an animal, a tree, a stone, or other such things.

Sri Balasai Baba

Devotee: *How can we be on the safe side?*

BABA: We need to believe in God. To realize His love, we need to run after Him, try to catch Him. With our thoughts, our deeds and our hearts, we should run on His tracks. If we think of God, God will automatically think of us. If we lay our lives down at His feet, then all His infinite love, His borderless grace, everything that He has to give will flow towards us without hindrance. We will be protected by Him and we will attain wisdom, enlightenment and liberation.

Devotee: *If somebody does something bad, will God punish him for that?*

BABA: **God does not need to punish you. You will be punished by the karmic law of cause and effect. You will harvest what you sow. Sow good things so that you will harvest good things. If you sow bad things, then you will harvest bad things.**

Devotee: *Could we fall back to the level of the animal?*

BABA: You could even regress back beyond the level of an animal. If you kill a dog in this life, then that dog might come back in the next life and kill you. A dog is also God.
The human can sink to the level of an animal, but he is also able to progress to the level of divinity.

Devotee: *Will there be an effect on my karma if I deliberately do something bad?*

BABA: If we know about the consequences of our actions, then we also carry the responsibility for those actions. But our actions can also have an unintended effect on our karma.
There was once a wise man who had acquired spiritual powers throughout his holy life. He had acquired direct access to God. As a five

year-old, he often played with dragonflies. One day he was tightening a thread around a dragonfly's tail and snapped the creature's tail by accident.

He had forgotten the incident by the time he had reached old age. When he was fifty or sixty, he was asked by the king to come to the royal court and talk of spiritual topics. The king did not like the lectures; he became furious. He ordered one of his soldiers to make the wise man sit on a trident. The wise man was in agony for eleven days and on the twelfth day he died.

When he arrived in heaven and had the opportunity to talk with God, he blamed God for giving him a cruel death after having lived his life reverently and peacefully. God responded, "Do you remember when you were five years old and you were torturing the dragonflies? That death is your reward for what you did." The man replied, "But as a child I did not know what I did!" "But you still did it; you must accept the consequences of your actions," God replied. Karma is karma; bad karma stands as a debt that has to be balanced.

Whether you do something bad deliberately or unknowingly, you will still reap the results. But accordingly, whether you do something good deliberately or unknowingly, you will similarly reap the results.

Once upon a time lived an orthodox, well-established, pious couple of Brahmans. They had a single son, whom they loved and pampered to an excessive degree. The older the son became, the more naughty he was. He hung around in the street, waiting to attack and rape innocents.
One day, while he was playing cards, some people, suspecting him of

theft, came and chased him through the streets. He narrowly escaped, finding shelter in an ancient temple of Shiva where a holy festival had just been celebrated. There he sat down silently in a corner. He sat there, still as a mouse so as not to attract attention to himself. In this way he escaped from his pursuers.

When the festival was finished and everybody had gone home, only the temple security guards stayed back. The guards laid down blessed gifts of food in front of the symbol of Shiva's symbol. The wicked man crept to the food in hopes of getting something to eat. But as soon as he had reached his goal, he accidentally knocked over a candle, alerting the guards of his presence.

Frightened, the intruder lost his balance. His forehead landed on Shiva's symbol. Instead of the usual offering of water, the man gave Shiva his blood. In this way he landed directly in Shiva's holy kingdom, where Shiva made him a ruler and protector of worlds. He became a God who ruled over the treasures and richness in the entire universe.

What is the moral of this story? Everything that happened to the man on the day of his death transpired without his awareness or consciousness. Unintentionally, he fasted that night, sung bhajans and gave Shiva his blood.

Devotee: *How do I get rid of bad karma?*
BABA: Do not kill any living creature. Kill your personal bad karma! For that there exists only one weapon: Pray from the depth of your heart! Concentrate on the name of God and on the form of God. Be joyful about any opportunity to do something good. With a sweet fragrance you can push away bad odor.

God is responding

Everything that happens to us occurs within the framework of karmic law. God created an unwritten law that we call destiny. Not even God Himself can do away with this law. **I also have to respect the laws of dharma and karma.**

Devotee: Baba, do you change our karma?

BABA: Why would I do that? You would only have to deal with your karma in another life. **If you get the chance to receive my blessings, you will have enough strength to face all your problems; you won't even perceive them as problems any more.** If you develop trust in me, I will give you my full blessing.

Devotee: Therefore it would be better if we in the West were to learn to accept our destiny, instead of seeking causes for everything?

BABA: Karma is the cause behind everything that happens. Therefore, you should not ask me to take away bad karma. Pray and ask that I bestow you with the power to accept the consequences of your actions with dignity. **Pay attention to your karma!** With good karma you can correct your old misdeeds. Then your next life will be better.

Devotee: You said earlier that you have saved someone's life. But you just said that you do not intervene in karmic law. How can we understand this?

BABA: If someone has dedicated completely his life to God and lives only for God, God will take over the karma of this person and remove him from the cycle of rebirths.

Devotee: Baba, why was I born in the West?

BABA: Your thoughts at the moment of death can determine the circumstances of your next birth. **For God there is no separation**

between East, West, North and South. For Him, all countries of the world are one. God loves all creatures. The entire world belongs to him. Only human beings create borders and want to be separated from each other.

In your home country a lot of people do not believe in rebirth. They are convinced that there is only a single life in which they have the unique chance to enjoy the pleasures of worldly existence. There is no time left for God. They think that when they die, everything will be over.

Devotee: *Baba, for we Westerners, the concept of karma is hard to comprehend. I know that your Indian devotees do not ask such questions as we do.*

BABA: They accept their karma, but they make a lot of effort to get my blessings so that they will have the power they need to do good things in this life and meet their fate with indifference. If you the people from the West cannot accept the concept of karma, then simply think: "I should always do something good." That is sufficient.

Devotee: *Can we only affect our karma as long as we are on earth?*

BABA: Yes. Only on earth can you change your karma. Until you achieve liberation, you must come and go. Up in heaven there is no work for you. Your karma controls your life. You cannot evade it, flatter it, or bribe it. Karma consists of cause and effect - action and reaction. You cannot manipulate it. It exerts its power over you without hesitation.

There was once a devotee who remained alone his entire life. God was his only true companion. Before taking a glass of tea in his hand he thanked God for it. As he grew old, his body decayed, but in his heart he stayed young. He had always been thinking of God. Only the body submits to decay. The heart stays eternally young if it is committed to God.

When the man grew old, he suffered from bad diarrhea. The constant diarrhea completely sapped his strength. Somebody had to come and clean him from top to bottom. Every day this person did this without being asked, demanding nothing in return. One day the old man recognized that this person was God. He put his hands together and begged, "Please give me the power to take care of myself. You should not do these impure things; I am quite ashamed."

But God responded: "This I am certainly not going to do, for I love you. If you want to be still able to act, then you will need to come back in a new body. This I do not want. If I heal you, then you need to come back." God served him until he died. With grace and clemency, He ended the karmic cycle of his loyal devotee.

Devotee: Can I leave everything up to karma?

BABA: We should not leave everything up to karma and up to God. We should always try to do our best and put our abilities to good use. **The fruits of our action we need to give to God, but we should not be insensible to the fruits of our actions.**

Devotee: Baba, I would like to get to know how the first bad karma came to be.

BABA: At the beginning you were clean, like a sheet of white paper. God gave you free will. When you became aware of your survival instincts, you started to do bad things. In the Bible, God said to Eve that she should not eat the fruit, but she did it anyway. You should not kill, but you kill anyway. Although you know what is bad, you repeat the same stupidity again and again. Because you are unconscious and unaware, you do all these things.

God gave you life and karma began. Karma does not mean anything other than action and thought and the effects of that action and thought. Karma means work. If you perform good work, then you will earn good fruits. If you do bad work, then you will earn bad fruits. The meaning of karma is itself neutral. It is you who determines whether it will be bad or good. Karma is like a white sheet. You can paint it however you please. **You cannot avoid your karma. It controls you completely.**

Devotee: Why are we bound to karma?

BABA: Karma is time itself! You are bound to karma as night follows day.

Devotee: A lot of people run away from their problems. Are they trying to escape their karma? What kind of advice can you give them?

BABA: Running away does not work. **You cannot avoid your karma. Living means that we must face problems.** Problems mean that we live! If there aren't any problems, then there is no karma; we are not bound to the wheel of rebirth any more. **By creating good karma, we can get rid of the bad results of our former actions.** We should never feel sorry for ourselves if we have accumulated bad karma. On the contrary, we should get out by asking for God's blessings, by doing good things and always thinking of Him, repeating His name.

God is responding

Devotee: Can thoughts also affect karma?

BABA: Your brain functions accordingly to your karma. Every event in your life has been brought about by way of your good or bad actions. Likewise, a single thought is the fruit that you have sown in former times.

Devotee: What about our parents?

BABA: We do not belong to our parents. We belong to the law of karma. That is what determines the circumstances of our birth.

Devotee: What about the animals, Baba?

BABA: Everything lives by karma. Every single living creature goes through the karmic cycle.

Devotee: But this means that for them, the circle of birth and death will never end- animals are always killing each other in order to survive.

BABA: Therefore, the life of a human is precious. After many cycles of birth and death, you receive the gift of a human body. Only as a human can you dedicate yourself wholeheartedly to God. You can decide to love, to use no violence, to be righteous and peaceful and to always speak the truth. It is truly a gift to be born as a human. Once you are there, you should not allow yourself to fall once again to lower levels of existence.

Devotee: And if God descends to the physical world in the form of a human being, does he also submit himself to karmic law?

BABA: When Sri Krishna knew that he had fulfilled the objective of his incarnation and that he was about to leave the earth, he went into a forest and laid down under a tree. A hunter passed and saw Sri

Krishna's tooth. He confused the tooth with a foot of a rabbit and shot an arrow into it.

The hunter rushed to him, recognized Krishna, knelt down in front of him and begged repentantly for his grace. But Krishna smiled and assured the hunter that he had not do anything bad and that Krishna was subject only to the unwritten karmic law. In his previous incarnation as Sri Rama, he had killed that same hunter by shooting him with an arrow. So even Sri Krishna lived and died according to his karma.

Devotee: *What if we have acted erroneously in the past, but now we cannot remember what we have done?*

BABA: **We do not need to know about our former bad deeds. We only need the courage to face our karma. When we pray to Baba, he will give us the strength we need to accept our fate. With good deeds, we can balance out our bad karma. Through Baba we get protection and courage.**

Devotee: *Baba, when I went into the city recently, I saw a rickshaw driver beating a donkey, hurting it badly. Is it enough for me to pray for divine intervention?*

BABA: What you describe is karma in action. Both the donkey and the rickshaw driver have to settle their karmic balance. You are only the witness. It is good when you pray to God, since He can intervene in countless ways. But if you yourself are able to help, that is even better. God will be happy to see you helping; He will stand by your side. **You should be always inclined to do and give your best in all situations.**

God is responding

L

LIBERATION

Devotee: *Please, Baba, tell us what liberation means.*

BABA: To be liberated means that your heart and the heart of Baba melt together. At the beginning of your journey, you open your heart. When you have advanced far enough, a master comes to you. You pray in your heart and with time the feeling of merging with your master will come and go. The greater your desire for God becomes, the more intense your thoughts and prayers will be. Then you become one with him.

You can observe this process in the physical world. Two people meet each other and feel mutually attracted. They go out together, fall in love with each other and finally two bodies become one. The spiritual process of becoming one with God is similar. At the end the devotee of God becomes one with the object of devotion. The atman, the limited self, merges into the paramatman, the unlimited universal soul.

Devotee: *Baba, what will happen if I ultimately merge with God?*

BABA: Inexhaustible bliss! You will not be separated from God anymore - and this is very beautiful.

Devotee: *Can Baba not grant us liberation?*

BABA: Do you trust me? Do you believe that I can present you with something like that?

Devotee: *(silence)*

BABA: Do you ask me to give you liberation to you alone? Or to others as well? And if all humans are liberated, who will then see to the continuity of the human race?

Devotee: *(silence)*

BABA: If you seek liberation, you should first go into yourself. Follow your inner heart and listen to what it tells you. Liberation is not just another nine-letter word. To make it a reality is not easy. But there are ways to take you to me more quickly.

Devotee: And what are they?

BABA: You should work on the refinement of your character, destroy your little ego and try to do things which God likes. If God did everything for you, where would you be? You need to do your best; God will bless you and support your efforts. God is a mute witness of your actions. If He sees that you make efforts to make Him happy, His heart will melt and He will shower silent blessings over you.

There are so many schools and ashrams where such spiritual techniques as yoga and pranayama *(breathing exercises)* are taught. Do you really need these on your way to God? **What do you really want? You want to become one with him. What do you need for that? Love and devotion.** God is ready to give you everything, but you have to be ready to receive.

If you want to find me you need to put my teachings into practice. Repeat the names of God, sing bhajans and meditate on me.

Then the cosmic veil of illusion will be torn apart and you will recognize who you really are. God Himself has thrown you into this world of illusion. As long as you are a prisoner of it, you move away from Him. The illusion remains until you reestablish an unbreakable connection with God. Then you are one with Him.

Devotee: *God can liberate us from illusion?*
BABA: When a child is little, it will always seek the hand of its parents for reassurance. On the spiritual path it is the same. **Every person is like a child that Baba must teach. At the beginning of the path, He gives his children a chocolate to make them happy and to let them grow spiritually.** To become a spiritual adult I tell people to meditate on Baba with each inhalation and exhalation. They must be constantly aware of his form and his name. **It is important that you concentrate on Baba. This leads you quickly to your goal.**

When it rains, it rains over the entire land. Rain knows no borders. To collect rainwater, you need to open your hands, form them into the shape of a bowl and catch the raindrops. God's love flows like rainwater. You need to be open to His love. The love of God is infinitely sweet. No worldly love can give you the slightest idea of what God's love is like.

To get in touch with God, we need only say His name! To repeat His name is a very practical exercise. It brings you much closer to God.

To be one with God is the highest objective. For this you need to work. Even if you live to be a hundred years old, you should not lose sight of your objective, even until your last breath. Your objective is to be one with God. You should always stick to that. Your thoughts should be directed towards oneness with God. **You should not worry about your past or your future. Concentrate on the present.**

Devotee: Could I merge with God in a single lifetime?

BABA: If you think that it is possible for you, then it is. It all depends on the intensity of your aspiration for God. If you have yearned for God in many past lives, it is possible to bundle all that yearning into a single life. Then you will want to live for God alone; you will not have any other wishes anymore.

Devotee: Do I have to use my will to achieve liberation, or will God give me what I seek?

BABA: The way to liberation is not an easy path. Two things are worth fighting for: happiness and liberation. Because neither comes to us automatically, we have to fight for them. We have to burn blazingly and direct all our energies on that. If a man makes one step towards me, then I will come one hundred steps closer to him. **If you first put forth your own efforts, then God will approach you.** If a human yearns for the presence of God, then he will become a child and stay ever by His side. The genuine yearning of a heart full of devotion opens the door. Once God is there, He will never go away, even if He is forsaken.

When you follow my instructions and make an effort, then my grace will be with you. It is not easy to attain liberation. Our mind creates difficulties. We stumble and fail to achieve our objective. But if you employ great willpower and efforts, then God will show you mercy. Without God's grace there is no chance to reach liberation. If boredom overcomes you, then look for good company, people who are focused on God. Do not waste your time with useless actions. You could write down or read the teachings I give you.

It is mentioned in all religions that it is not easy to reach God; only through sufferings and efforts you can reach Him. But if you accept everything that happens with an open mind and heart, then the way is very simple and easy. For others it may seem that you are suffering, but you are not going to perceive it as suffering, since you do everything for the love of Baba and therefore joyfully accept everything that you encounter. If you follow my words, then your liberation will be assured.

You should not think, "I could fail in my quest for liberation." Concentrate on your goal with firm belief in your ability to achieve it. Let your thoughts be uplifting. Love me more and more. I will likewise love you more and more and it will automatically happen that I melt with you. Whatever you feel, think, say and do – God will feel, think, say and do. He is your mirror.

Devotee: *So how can I pursue liberation?*

BABA: First, we have to make up our minds about what we want in life. Then we must decide to pursue our goals. If we know someone from whom we can learn the way to liberation, we should follow. But it takes time to ponder and to decide. Take your time. Your inner voice will guide you.

Like water and soap cleans the body, the divine form cleans your soul. With the same attention that you take care of your body, you should look after your soul. The efforts that you dedicate to your family or your work should be dedicated to God. We must cry out for God, like a six month old baby crying its soul out until the mother finally comes and puts it to her breast.

Sri Balasai Baba

In order to achieve union with God, your mind, body and thought must all work together. Nowadays, these three elements travel in different directions. There is no unity between them. Once they are united, you can focus your energies on God.

I will tell you a story. Once upon a time, a fox came to God. When God asked him what he wanted, the fox said, "I want not to be hungry anymore. I do not want to have to hunt anymore." God warned the fox, saying, "Be careful what you wish for." But the fox replied, "I am sure that this is what I want! This is my greatest wish!"

So God granted the fox's wish. The fox went back into the forest and was not hungry from then on. He saw others busy doing their work. They hunted, ate and slept, all together. Soon he was alone and there was nothing that he could do. It was terribly boring for him and he suffered greatly. He again went to God, who gave him another chance to ask for something. "Well, what do you really want?" asked God. "Liberation!" the fox replied. In the end, the fox got his liberation.

If you truly seek liberation, then this wish should become your sole goal, the main objective in your life. All your actions should be directed towards the pursuit of this lofty goal. Body, spirit and soul may not be separately directed towards liberation; they are all interconnected. If we have performed good deeds in the last life and therefore are able to think about God, we have the desire for liberation – liberation from the infinite cycles of rebirths and deaths.

LIFE

Devotee: *And what should be my attitude towards life?*

BABA: Much happens in the life of a human being. Some people call what happens karma. Others call it destiny or fate. Others call it the will of God. Whatever happens, let it happen! A smart person will know that whatever may happen, whatever he might feel, it is the will of God. Everything comes from God: Joy and sadness, profit and loss. God gives and God takes away. If you are able to think in this manner, then you will be truly free!

Devotee: *And how can I understand my own life?*

BABA: Life is very short. You should spend the rest of your life joyfully, happily and in love. Walk on the trail of God, the good path. If you think too much about the past or the future, then you will age quickly and your life will become painful. Let your sorrows go and be happy! Sorrow is followed by joy and joy is followed by sorrow. If you meet both conditions indifferently, then you will be free and you can stay happy. Whatever comes is sent by Baba. If it is good, then say: "Thank you, Baba!" And if it is bad then also say "Thank you Baba!" Let everything happen and know that whatever happens is for the best.

Devotee: *Baba, how can we human beings lead a sensible life?*

BABA: Once you recognize that everything is God, you can lead a totally normal life. You can practice any profession, marry, have children and be healthy and rich. **But you should live in the awareness that God is omnipresent; you should dedicate part of your time to Him.**

Whatever you do in your life, meditate and think about God. Present God your heart, for it is He who gave you this life. When you marry, venerate your wife or husband as a manifestation of the divine. Regard him or her as God.

There was once a devotee who arrived in heaven at the same time as a prostitute. When God appeared, the devotee complained about the presence of the prostitute. God replied: "This prostitute sacrificed her body to men to earn her living. While she was working, she devoted herself entirely to Me. She thought only of Me. She was so intensely concentrated that she was not even aware who came to her. She has suffered much and deserves respect."

Devotee: *What is the real reason for the creation of the universe?*

BABA: There is none. It is a game. If you have a child, you buy it many toys. It plays with them a while. Then when it does not want them any more, you put them away. It will be like that on earth when everything is over.

Devotee: *Is the realization of God also a game?*

BABA: The realization of God means winning the game. Your goal is to be happy.

Devotee: *What is the meaning of life?*

BABA: In public discourse this same topic is treated over and over again: What is the goal of existence? What is the meaning of life? But everyone must discover this for himself or herself. If somebody else is hungry, can you then eat for him? Will his stomach be full, when you have filled yours? Everybody needs to eat his or her own meal. Similarly, everyone must find a path of his or her own. Baba will always

show the way – but you have to walk it yourself.

LOVE

Devotee: Baba, what is love?

BABA: **Real love demands that we give up the arbitrary borders of ego and family and develop love towards all beings. We should not only see our own happiness, but also the happiness of all beings. We need to make strong efforts to live together in peace and harmony. When you pray to God, ask that He blesses your fellow humans with the same grace that you ask for yourself.**

Love is something very holy and virtuous. Love wants only to give. Even if it rains bombs, you may not stop your decision to love. If necessary, you should even be ready to die for divine love. But your ordinary love - I mean what most people call love – is really only sex. It is not truly divine love. It is selfish love. Only if you stay together through poverty, sickness, unhappiness and bad conditions can you talk about true love. The love of the mother is the greatest type of human love. But the love of God is a thousand times greater.

I love you! – Only God and your mother can truly say this, because only they love you truly. Beloved ones, husbands and wives should say, "I like you," because their love is not necessarily permanent. It only stays vivid as long as their mutual expectations are fulfilled. True love is something virtuous and pure. It gives without taking. Love, love, love and always only love. Pure love is the highest that exists. All we want is love. I embrace and kiss a leper, if he loves me.

Devotee: Baba, my mother has never loved me.

BABA *(made her repeat the statement and then looked at her a long time.)*: It is like that because between you and your mother there was never a real relationship. If you want to be loved, start to love and then the love will come back.

You are now carrying a bag full of useless personal matters. In order to fill it with my treasures, you need to empty those bags. Forget your past and do not worry about the future. Live now.

Take my hand; I will lead you. I am ready to give you everything, but you have to be ready to take it. When I want to pour something into your hand, you have to open it first. How can you receive my present if your palm is facing the floor?

Devotee: I thought about the meaning of love and concluded that I do not know what love is. Could you help me?

BABA: There are so many types of love. There is love between man and woman. The love between mother and father and their children has another quality. The love between sister and brother is another type of love. The love in all these relationships is based on expectations. From your sister you do not expect the same as from your husband and from your father you expect something other than the love you get from your mother.

Loving God is completely different, because physical proximity is not an issue. Your love for God flows through your heart and through your thoughts. Then you experience true love and true

joy. This particular feeling you cannot share with anybody else. It belongs to you alone. Others might say that you became crazy, because they cannot share your experiences. **Love is very holy; it does not expect or demand anything. Love flows freely, it only gives. It does not take anything.**

To love is a creative deed, in contrast to the hatred that creates destruction. Apathy brings about death. Lack of love brings about solitude. An absence of love generates a desert in the heart. The greenery of life shrivels. Love is the absolute power, necessary for human existence. **Love originates from natural sources. On its way into the divine light it dreams of a great world. Selflessness is the true shield of love.** From love springs contentment.

Devotee: And when I love?

BABA: If we love, we will be loved. Only through love can we find the way to God. Without love, nothing can exist in this universe. God has given us a lot of ways to find Him. Love each other. Then there will be no hatred between you. Your heart should pure and invincible. I only want your holiness of your heart, not your body or your material possessions.

Devotee: And your love for us?

BABA: The ways in which I bestow you love have nothing to do with your expectations. I do everything because I love you. I am the doctor and you are the patient. I know what you need. The heart of the human beats differently than my heart does. My heart beats: Love, love, love and only love.

Devotee: *How can we love all humans equally?*

BABA: See all humans as your own relatives, for you are only able to love what you see as your own.

Devotee: *Jesus taught that we should love our enemies as ourselves. What do you say about that?*

BABA: Nowadays you are incapable even of loving your own children, your own brothers and sisters! If your child cries, you are immediately irritated, you lose control and you yell at your child. Yes, Jesus said that you should love your enemies. But this was two thousand years ago. Today my message is: **Try to love yourself. A lot of time passes before you can accept yourself completely. Only then can you love.**

You waste your precious time pointlessly thinking about this or that enemy. Save your time and energy and devote yourself to God. This alone will help you. Energy can be wasted so easily; it can dissipate and scatter in all directions. Try to get it back and concentrate it on God.

Devotee: *How can I love God?*

BABA: The first step on the way to God is the opening of the thick door of your closed heart. **Try to meet God as your master.** If you create a place in your heart for God, then He will reply with all embracing love. Love is not a one-way street. If you love Him, then He will love you. If you love Him more, then He will love you more and more.

God is responding

M

MANTRA

Devotee*: What kind of mantra should be chosen by your adherents to remind themselves constantly of you?*

BABA: It is "Om Balasai Ram", which means: Welcome our God Sai Ram. If you need a mantra, you can also repeat constantly, "I do not want to be reborn in another life. I want to attain unity with God."

The mantra that you repeat is up to you. For instance, you can repeat one of the following mantras: "Om Sri Balasai Ram, Om Sri Balasai Namaha, Om Namo Bhagavate Sri Balasai Babaya." You can also try to become intuitively aware of my form by concentrating on my photograph. **Put up a photo of me at home. That will not only protect you from people with bad thoughts and intentions, but it will also guarantee my personal presence. If my photo is in your house, I am also present in reality.**

Devotee: *Is it important to know all 300 names of God?*

BABA: *(Baba opens a book with names of God)*. Choose the name of God that you like the most. This is name that you are going to speak in your mind, whispering it silently or even loudly. You will see the form that you have chosen. Remember that God is truly formless, but from time to time His physical presence on earth is necessary. He listens to prayers of the people and incarnates because of their love for Him.

Sri Balasai Baba

A woman once came to me and uttered only a single word: "difficulties." So I told her: **If you constantly repeat the word difficulties, then you will undoubtedly get more difficulties. Thinking negative thoughts will be just as harmful as saying negative things. Instead of saying the long word, "difficulties," say a short name of God, like "Baba," or "Balasai."** If you repeat the divine name and you devote yourself to God, then you will procure God's blessings and grace.

Devotee: Why should we repeat the name of God?

BABA: Today's generation is mentally polluted. Constantly repeating the name of God is one of the best ways to remove that pollution, layer by layer. One needs a great amount of patience before an effect can be perceived. Pray every day to me with a loving heart. Concentrate on my form and my name. **If you pray regularly, with a full heart and with the utmost concentration, you should be able to perceive the positive and cleansing effect of your exercise.** This exercise pulls you out of the swamp in which you got stuck and from which you seek liberation. **Merging with God requires a sacrifice of time and energy. You must practice meditation, the recitation of names and the singing of bhajans.**

Constantly falling drops hollow out a rock. As water constantly falling on the same spot makes a hole in the rock, so you should be persistent with your meditation. Little by little, progress can be made. If this is not possible for you, then you should work on your consciousness.

MARRIAGE

Devotee: *What can you tell us about the relationship between two human beings?*

BABA: A relationship between two people is like two tree trunks floating down a river. They float together for a while until the current separates them. This is what happens to human beings. You can never know how long your relationship will last. The tree trunk image connotes the inconstancy of their relationships. You chain yourself to husband, mother, father, sister, brother and friends. You forget to dedicate part of your time to God. Your bondage makes you come and go from one reincarnation to another. This is terrible. If you are in danger and you need help, will you cry for your husband, father or mother? What can they do for you? They will simply mourn and pour out tears. Tie yourself to God; liberate yourself from worldly chains.

I have given you each other so that you can be happy. For that you should be grateful. Without man there can be no woman. Without woman, no man. You belong together; you are one body. The right hand helps the left hand and the left hand helps the right hand (*Baba looks at a statue of the god Ardhanarishware - God in half male and half female form*). Man and woman should be like the right and left wheel of a two-wheeled carriage. God is the driver; they should follow him readily.

Devotee: *What does this mean for somebody who is married?*

BABA: You must dedicate yourself to God before you marry; then there won't be any problems. Then when you are married you have to fulfill your duties as a head of the household, father or mother.

Devotee: *In marriage, what duties does the husband have?*

BABA: He should be ready to carry his wife's burdens until his death. He should be able to always stay with her and give her whatever she needs. Many husbands nowadays do not want to accept any responsibility. Here in India, the priest prays at the wedding, "If you work and if you perform your duty, then I will be with you. In the moment of your liberation I won't leave you." The bridegroom promises to perform these duties, but what will happen later, we do not know.

In this universe there is only one being who can give you everlasting happiness and that is the husband of the entire universe. No lover, no husband, no drug can put you in the ecstatic state that God's love can. God's love cannot be described with words. It is eternally sweet and everlasting.

If you are married, then your husband might have a right to your body, but you alone are responsible for your thoughts and feelings; only you can control them. Nobody else can do that for you, not even God. You can only ask that He might help you.

We do not need to be dependent on anybody. We can retain our inner freedom and stand on our own two feet. If we are dependent on someone else, always expecting something of them, then pain and suffering will always be lurking just around the corner.

Devotee: When I first came to Baba two years ago, I led a useless and wasteful life. My life was full of meaningless distractions, like food and alcohol. I was not always nice to my two children or my wife, but they supported me patiently. Baba scolded me for my inhuman and unjust behavior. He said that I should repeat his names and concentrate on his form. I followed his words and experienced change. Today there is peace and joy in my heart and in my thoughts. I am happiest when I can concentrate completely on Baba. I have learnt to behave lovingly towards my wife and my children.

BABA: It is your duty to love your children as a father. How will they eventually love their own children if you haven't showed them how to love?

Devotee: What should we name our child, Baba?

BABA: It should be called Balasai. If you want to have children and you are fully devoted to me, then I will personally come into your house in the form of this child. Balasai is a divine name. Everybody has the right to give his child this name. You do not need special permission. Whether they are boys or girls, children who bear this name will be blessed. My name is a mantra – a holy word. Those children who have this name already manifest divine vibrations. This is very good for their futures. They will have good lives.

Children with that name will be awake, interested and spiritual. They are going to live easy and joyful lives. They will joyfully serve the people who need help. They will be very successful, no matter what they do. They will be a blessing to their fellow human beings. They will be a blessing for society and for their parents. These children possess an extraordinary capacity for concentration. They may be skilled in chemistry, biology, medicine and also in the fine arts. They are going to use their skills for the benefit of the society.

MATERIAL GOODS

Devotee: Can you say something about our relationship with the material world?

BABA: Nowadays people are addicted to the physical and material world. They fill their lives with sensual pleasures. Then they become old and die. How tragic is that! **Those who do this have not noticed that God has been waiting for all these years, ready and waiting to give permanent and divine bliss.** Life is very short. Awaken at last! Recognize that your true nature is divine. God dwells in you. Open your heart and your mind to this miraculous fact!

Human beings do not want to know about God. When they come to me, they mostly want material goods. They ask for money, houses, marriages, gold, rings and the like. They do not want God. This is very tragic. If you have an urgent desire and you are happy when I fulfill it, then I am also happy. But you should carefully think about what you wish from me, since God gives you what you have asked of Him. Be careful what you wish for.

Do not waste your time! Be busy with good actions, good thoughts and good feelings. Think of God, even if you are here, physically close to God. The obsession with material success automatically pushes you away from God and leads you back to the world of matter. Be content with what you already possess. Do not long for more. **Those who are grateful for each tiny item will receive more and more. A grateful heart rejoices in God. It makes Him happy to shower**

God is responding

the grateful with gifts.

There are people to whom God can give eternally, but who will always be dissatisfied and complain. Then God knows: "Whatever I give this person, he is never happy and content. He does not appreciate my abilities. My efforts to make him happy are not helping him. Thus, I will leave everything up to him from now on."

Even if you possess everything in the mundane world, if you have lost God, then you will be the poorest person in the entire universe. If you possess God, then you will be the wealthiest man in the universe.

I will tell you a story. There was once a king who lived in Rajasthan. He started to build a fortress there. For this project thousand of helpers had to be employed. One day he stepped on the balcony of his palace and gazed with pride on the multitude working for him. 'I am very powerful,' he thought.

When he went back to the palace, the divine mother Kali was already waiting for him. She asked him, 'Did you forget that I only use you as my instrument? Did you forget that it was I who gave you all this money and power and that nothing belongs to you?' The king immediately regretted his thoughts and asked Kali for forgiveness.

The story should help you to understand how it is crucial for humans to serve God with devotion. You always have to think: It is not me who acts; it is God. Everything comes from Him and everything belongs to Him. If you throw coins into a beggar's pot, you need to think that it is God that throws the money.

Sri Balasai Baba

Devotee: A lot of people seek to live a purely spiritual existence. They think that they do not need to do anything in the material world anymore.

BABA: Maybe. But it is not good if you thereby become lazy. **God does not like laziness.** Those who fail in the material world also have difficulties on the spiritual path. God has created contrasts - light and shadow, good and bad, hot and cold, man and woman and likewise matter and spirit. The spirit rules over the matter, but the human consists of both matter and spirit.

We must not become lazy in the name of spirituality. Think of me when you work. It is good to work and to earn your own living; do not depend on others. Do not shirk your material duties! You should be able to stand on your own feet and require no help from others. If you are remiss in your worldly duties, you and your family will suffer. For you nobody should have compassion. I want to make you inwardly and outwardly strong. I want you to be self-reliant and free.

And do not idle away the hours here at the ashram. Spiritual practice requires effort, not laziness. Work and earn your living and dedicate the rest of your time to God. Idleness leads to boredom; boredom leads to bad habits.

Be good karma warriors! Work is service to God. We can only expect something if we work. We must give if we expect to receive.

The problem with humans is that they not only become entangled in relationships, but they are also bound to their possessions and transitory things. You can and you may possess everything, but you have to forget what you have. If your ego gets involved, if you become attached to your worldly possessions, the results will be extremely tragic. Put everything down at the feet of God and accept everything that life brings.

In former times, it was taught that you must renounce the material world in order to achieve liberation. They taught that you had to suffer. I am telling you today: That is nonsense. You have to first be happy in the material world. That will give you the preparation you need to be spiritually successful.

We can realize God happily and joyfully. We derive no benefit from sadness. I do not tell people to leave everything and live only a spiritual monastic life. The few who make that choice should stick with it, but people who live in the world of matter can stay there and still be on the spiritual path. By taking action in the material world, they can neutralize their bad karma. And by being on the spiritual path they can accumulate good karma for their next life. It is good to live both on the material and the spiritual planes.

MEDITATION

Devotee: *Baba, how should we go about meditating?*

BABA: First, sit in a meditative position with your eyes closed. Try to picture Baba in your mind. Concentrate on Baba's name and on the form of Baba. This yields joy and good results. The repetition of Baba's name connects you immediately to the source. If you want to make a phone call, you have to dial the number first. If you want to write a letter, you have to mark the right address so that the postman can deliver the letter. It is similar with my name.

Later on, you will be able to visualize Baba's form everywhere. Do not think that there exists a place where Baba does not exist. He is everywhere.

A lot of people believe that meditation means that they need to sit on at particular site and in a particular posture, focusing on a particular part of the body. **However, true meditation means that you constantly remember God and concentrate on it. Do not forsake that name and form for one second. Then you can meditate in each position: lying, standing, walking and sitting.**

Devotee: Can we meditate anywhere? For example, can we meditate while washing, walking and eating? Will be the effect always the same if we are meditating with concentration?

BABA: Yes, of course. Every action depends on the applied concentration. Everything that you do for God is equally good. And the things that you do in His name are meditations.

But it is crucial that you stick to one form of God, like Shiva, Rama, Krishna, Buddha, Christ, or Shirdi Sai Baba. They are all avatars of love. **They came to earth in order to bring the people a pure and selfless love.** All religions lead to the same goal: The realization of God. Hence you should choose the form that you love most.

Devotee: Should we meditate alone, or in a group?

BABA: If you really meditate and concentrate totally on God, then you can do whatever you please. But if you fall asleep when you try to meditate alone, that is a problem. In that case it is better to meditate in a group. The outcome will be better. Look, it is very simple. Imagine that this is a company. Is it better for company employees to work together or separately? It is the same here.

Devotee: *Is it better to meditate silently or with a mantra?*

BABA: This depends upon what you like best. If you are happy with a silent meditation, then be silent. If you are happy with a mantra meditation, then meditate with a mantra. **The main point is that you concentrate on God. This alone is the goal of all spiritual practices.**

Whenever you have time, meditate! If you think about God, it strengthens your love for him. Do not simply sit during meditation.

As soon as you think of God, He will be there. Whenever you think of Him, pray to Him, meditate or sing to Him, He will stand behind you. I was very happy about your meditation. Your singing was so nice that I was drawn to this place and now I am sitting here.

Devotee: *Is there are a certain time that is best for meditation? If we meditate in the early morning hours, will this be more beneficial for us?*

BABA: If you live for God, you won't need a specific time to dedicate yourself to Him. **Most people only pray to God when they are sad or unhappy. They also pray when they want something - they pray for wisdom, spiritual powers, etc. These people should stick to certain times for meditation and prayer. Choose a certain hour every day for your meditation. Then you should sit down and meditate.**

If this practice is not yet sufficient, then when you take a shower or a bath, when you put on your clothing, repeat a set number of mantras as you perform these daily tasks. But it is important to repeat these mantras a certain number of times. If you decide to repeat a mantra 108 times, then you need to stick to the number 108. This practice gives you the stability that keeps you in balance.

Being in balance is very important. Look to nature; it shows you balance. The summer season comes in summer, the fall season comes in fall, the winter season comes in winter and the spring season comes in spring. Spring does not come in fall and summer does not come in winter. Your body is another example of balance. Finding this balance is the first step on the spiritual path. Later on, you can meditate whenever you find time.

Devotee: *When I meditate and I talk with you, how can I be sure that it is God who responds and not my own mind?*

BABA: If you truly believe that your mind belongs to God, then you will understand. If you think that God is God and you are you and that you are separated from each other, then you will put unnecessary obstacles in your way. But in fact you are one.

The most important thing is that you inwardly repeat the name of the Lord with devotion and love. Then chose the divine form that you love most and keep it alive before your inner eye.

Devotee: *How long should each meditation session last?*

BABA: There is no minimum or maximum time when it comes to meditation. For it does not matter what you do - it is always for yourself, not for God. Whether we hate or love, we only do it for ourselves. The more you do, the more that will happen. If you go to your office and work full-time, you will earn more money then you will if you work part-time. You spend a lot of time eating, but eating is for the body. Mediation is for the heart. Maintaining our heart should be as important to us as maintaining our body.

MIND

Devotee: *Should I listen to my mind or not?*

BABA: If we follow the whims and impulses of the mind, we will be like marionettes at the mercy of a puppeteer. Mental control requires concentration and spiritual practice. We should be masters of our feelings and our thoughts. They will always demand something new; they will never cease to look for change.

By constantly looking for ostensibly joyful experiences, the mind uses the body and keeps it busy seeking sensual satisfaction. You have to differentiate between pleasures that are ephemeral and those that are eternal. Physical pleasure comes and goes, for the body wants always to eat, drink, sleep and procreate. But more desires arise as soon as one is fulfilled. As soon as a man has eaten something he thinks: Let me still do this or that.

But if, however, you have prayed to God, you will say, "O this was nice. Let me pray again." That's how the body or the mind functions. The mouth exists not just for eating, but also for praying.

Devotee: *Baba, my mind is very jumpy. I cannot even concentrate for 20 minutes. After five minutes my mind begins running in all directions. What can I do about this?*

Sri Balasai Baba

BABA: You need to be very awake and observe your mind. You must not to allow it to run away. This mind is very tiny, but it dominates the big heavy body in an incredible way.

Use your mind to think as often as you can about Baba. If your thoughts fly away, spiritual practice can help you get them back. God gives you your mind, but He leaves it up to you how to handle it. You can switch it on or off. Thoughts come and go. When you think positively about others, then your thoughts come from God. But when you think negatively, then your thoughts stem from your little ego. But human beings tend to attribute good thoughts to themselves and bad thoughts to God. Exactly the opposite is true.

Imagine that your mind is a dog that leaves your house in the morning and returns in the evening. You could try to get it back yourself, or you could wait until it returns to you on its own. Which do you prefer?

One day the great Shankara prayed to the highest form of the divine mother. She asked him, "What do want from me?" Shankara responded: **"Please help me to better control my mind. It sometimes behaves like a flock of wild animals."** Even the great Shankara had to ask the divine mother for help. Even he, who could communicate with all forms of God, was not a master of his own thoughts and feelings. Be aware of that. You should never stop trying to tame your mind. Do not allow the fluctuations of your mind take power over you and rob you of your inner peace.

Another devotee: *Sometimes my head is completely empty.*

BABA: You mean that your thoughts are still? That is very good! Every spiritual practices aims for mental stillness. You are lucky; you experience this stillness without any special exercises.

Devotee: *How should we cope with our thoughts?*
BABA: Present them to me. I will throw them into the river.

MIRACLES

Devotee: *Why do you perform miracles, Baba?*
BABA: These days, people do not believe in God unless they see miracles. Performing these so-called miracles requires only a tiny part of our powers. To generate something out of nothing is not a big deal, but still people come to see miracles. Then, very slowly, they start to open themselves up to God. The moment will come when they truly start to believe.

I perform miracles so that you wonder and marvel. These miracles are visible expressions of the divine will. If you are truly God, then you shall be able to perform miracles. If a man claims to be a singer, how can we verify his claim? Only at last by hearing him singing something. By giving you outward evidence, I am trying to evoke an internal response.

I can perform any of the miracles described in the Bible or the Koran. If you believe that Jesus was able to perform miracles, then you can also believe me. **Everything that my hands touch becomes holy. What comes out of my hands is holy.**

Sri Balasai Baba

God is the greatest of all miracles. You can never enter the interior of my heart, but you should make great efforts to explore my perceptible qualities: all that you can see, hear and experience.

The divine incarnation carries the entire universe within Him; He possesses all powers and abilities - but He still keeps quiet and still. The human is made of nothing, does not know anything and also cannot do anything. Yet the human being is constantly proclaiming how great and terrific he is. All treasures, all knowledge, all power is in God, but God does not show it. He behaves quietly.

The amount of gold and silver that I have presented people over the years would fill trucks. Look, everyone who is sitting here possesses a golden ring from me. If I had been collecting all the materialized gold and silver I would have been a multi-millionaire.

A human gives and expects something. God is different. He is at all times ready to pour all the richness of the material and spiritual world over humanity without pondering how much He has given. God gives only out of love, like a mother who loves her children above everything. Whenever I give you something sweet, I bless you with a sweet heart.

Devotee *(doubting): Baba, are you a magician?*

BABA: Some people call me a magician. Do you know that Sri Krishna and Jesus Christ were also called magicians? A magician is somebody who carries out performances to earn money. Here the performance is the same but my goal is different. I perform in order to wake you up from your dull and profound sleep.

God is responding

You should not worry too much about miracles. They are only superficial catalysts; they are there to make you think. Concentrate on me, not on the miracles. If you focus only on miracles, there is the danger that you will become jealous of somebody who got some materialized items from me. Spirituality is most important.

When I was a small boy, a magician visited me. He said that he could make razorblades, snakes, lizards and long knives disappear down his throat. I said to him: "You kill lizards and snakes, but can you make them alive again? Only if you can make a dead thing come to life again, you do have the right to kill."

Devotee: *What is the meaning of this pink stone you have materialized?*

BABA: If you do not think of me, it will be only a piece of jewelry. If you think of me when you see the ring, I will immediately be with you and protect you. This stone in the ring shines like the lightning in the heavens. It means that your future will be full of light and joy. You will experience a lot of light in your life.

When I materialize a ring or precious stone, usually the recipient will simply say, "O, I am so blessed. Baba has created a ring and he has presented it to me." He will never ask me about the meaning of the ring itself. A ring is an auspicious symbol. It brings happiness to those who possess it. It is a talisman, a good luck charm. Whenever you see this ring, you will remember Baba and the good feelings you had when you received the ring from me. The ring also symbolizes goodwill!

Do not be frightened if the stone emanates light. A German monk was here and I gave him a ring. When he was back in Germany he showed it to a woman. When she looked at the stone a glaring light shot out.

This so affected her that she decided to come here.

Devotee: *Where do these materialized items come from?*

BABA: All these things stem from me and will someday return back to me. Everything in nature, even humanity, originates from me and finally merges with me. If a person accumulates good karma, they will someday find their way back to me.

Devotee: *Is this wonderful ring with the orange stone for me, Baba?*

BABA: Now you will always remember me. When you eat, when you write, when you do anything at all, you will see this ring and think: "Baba, please come." Then I will come. I am always with you, even if you are not aware of my presence all the time. Sometimes you will even be able to see me in the stone itself.

If someone asks you about the origin of the ring, you should tell the truth and leave it up to them to believe or not. A miracle is a miracle. Something is called a miracle because not everybody believes it. If everybody believed it, it would not be a miracle anymore.

Devotee: *Do you like miracles?*

BABA: The miracles simply happen. I cannot predict if a miracle will happen or not. I do not generate them. Everything depends upon the person and his or her karma. I do only my duty.

If you come to Balasai Baba to see miracles, then you will see miracles. If you come to Baba for a ring, then he will give you a ring. But this is very stupid of you, for God is very great and powerful. He is the treasurer, the treasury and the treasure. Therefore, think about what you want from God. Seek God in His entirety; then you will get everything.

In this darkest of the all epochs, people need to see miracles to believe in God. It is a pity, since God Himself is the greatest of all miracles.

MONEY

Devotee: *Can I take some money for my work?*

BABA: Without money, we cannot live. Even honoring God requires money. Therefore, you should not have any reservations about taking money for your work. It is wrong to do everything for free. This attitude promotes the inertia and laziness of human beings. Do you know a single shop where you can get a bar of chocolate for free? If there were such a shop, people would make a pilgrimage there every day for ten free chocolate bars. Since such a shop does not exist, they limit themselves to one bar of chocolate per week or month. Therefore, demand something for your work, otherwise you will attract sluggards who will stick to you like chewing gum.

If you take money for what you do, certain people will criticize you. If you do not take money, others will criticize you. Therefore, do not worry about criticism.

Devotee: *The Indians who have money often talk about their savings. Why?*

BABA: No money is a problem. Too much money is also a problem.

It destroys the human character. We always need to have enough money to eat, to have roof over our head and to buy clothes to wear. You can have a lot of money and property, but you should never think that it belongs to you. Being satisfied with what you have is central to a peaceful life.

Devotee: *If a man is quite rich, but uneducated, will the society then respect him?*

BABA: He might be uneducated, dirty, or even stricken by leprosy. If he is rich then the people will come and touch his feet. They will greatly respect him.

MORALITY

Devotee: *Can I rely on my intuition to tell me whether something is right or wrong?*

BABA: If you have put your life at the feet of God, you do not need to think about what is right or wrong. What you need to understand is that everything is God. You are only His instrument. Do not think that it is only you who acts. Can we consider an instrument to have character? God does everything through you; you do not exist. **To be aware that you are an instrument in the hand of God is not easy. It requires meditation.**

NATURE

Devotee: *Does nature speak a language?*

BABA: Nature is God - God is nature. **Nature is your best teacher.** If you learn to observe it profoundly and exactly, then you can recognize the greatness of God. **You can learn everything from nature; it is the greatest teacher.**

Every law of life can be found in nature. Look, now it is raining heavily. Lighting is flashing on the horizon and thunder rumbles in the distance. Heaven is pouring water down for the benefit of human beings. But how much pain is linked to it! The water arrives with a deafening noise.

Isn't it the same when a baby is born? The mother carries her child beneath her heart for nine months. Before it can reach the light, she must withstand terrible pains. So every birth is linked to labor pains –

(A sudden blackout occurs in the temple.) Look, the light is followed by darkness and darkness is followed by light. We should always be prepared for the darkness and for the light. Now we are sitting in the darkness and waiting for the light. Look at the candle. It sacrifices itself for us by burning selflessly and giving light until it is burnt down. For that it does not expect any benefit from us.

(Outside it continues raining.) Heaven does not want to stop weeping. Now it is getting rid of all its sorrows and shedding big tears. But by tomorrow it will be relieved and there will be cheerful peace.

Devotee: Baba, how is it that nature has sent us acid rain, dying fish, landslides and other such things?

BABA: **Nature is God. Every time you violate the laws of nature, nature will teach you a lesson in reaction.** Therefore, before you act you need to consult your intellect and first think about whether your action is beneficial or not.

Devotee: Very often we hear that the planet earth will not survive long. Is this true? Could you save the earth? Are there any other planets that are prepared to welcome us?

BABA: The planet earth won't perish, at least not so quickly. Those who believe in God will be protected by God. They will all survive in the event of a catastrophe. Those who do not believe will perish. Some believe that the end of the world is close, but they are wrong. On the other hand, it is true that those who do not have any human values will gradually disappear from this earth.

NIGHTMARES

Devotee: Why do we have to experience nightmares?

BABA: Only God is real; everything else is unreal. **If you cannot stand the darkness then you cannot stand the light!** God is everything! God is the light and God is the darkness!

Devotee: Why does God send me a horrible dream when I ask Him for help?

BABA: Your horrible dreams are not related to God; the dreams are produced by your frightened brain. If a devotee is terrified of the divine mother, how then can she appear in front of him? Even if she appeared in the guise of fear, he should praise her, saying, **"O mother, I know that You are only love!"** Then she will change into love and beauty and pour out her blessings.

Everything ugly and terrible is only a reflection of you. God is an impeccable mirror. If you think only positively about God and offer the good, then He will reflect the absolute beauty of heaven.

NON-VIOLENCE

Devotee: What about violence?

BABA: Violence is inhuman. Still, the birth of a human being shows that violence has a crucial role to play in the maintenance of the world. Non-violence is a highly evolved state of being. It is a purified way of thinking. Non-violence is the flood of light that changes darkness and violence into a cool, quiet and peaceful bed in which the individual can relax. But this relaxation does not mean that he is inactive. On the contrary, he should be internally active, peaceful but involved. **Non-violence is superior to violence on all levels. Devotees should integrate non-violence into their daily lives.**

Destructive action is the result of an unbalanced state of mind.

Creativity alone will sustain the universe. Violence has to be discouraged on all levels of life. It undermines the very foundation of humanity. **Where humanity ends, violence begins. A violent person loses the power of judgment and become like a wild animal.**

People should venerate all existence. They should praise the dust at their feet. I want my devotees to practice creative non-violence. This quality serves the country, the world and the entire universe. This avatar transforms the bad into the good, not through violence but through non-violent actions. Bad should be replaced by good. Your sense of duty will help you to do that.

P

PATIENCE

Devotee: How does one cultivate patience?

BABA: This is one of the most crucial exercises we can practice. Your progress can be measured by whether your life has become balanced and peaceful. If we have patience in life and do not expect anything, then we will be truly free!

To expect anything is not good, for if our expectations are not met, we will become depressed. On the other hand, if we get something that we expect, then our ego will enlarge, which is also bad. Therefore, we should stay neutral, accepting whatever comes up without expectation. Expectation leads you directly to inner unrest, to disappointments, anger and aggression. **To be free of expectations means to be free of disappointments. Simply do not expect anything!**

Your generation does not possess patience. If it were possible, you would eat with your ears in order to accelerate the process of eating. **By being agitated and impatient, you will kill yourself.** God gives you the gift of life and you throw it away by rushing around, smoking cigarettes and being impatient. God gave you fire to prepare food, not to light cigarettes or houses.

Why do you always have to move so fast? How will it benefit you? Before bicycles, motorcycles and cars were invented, people walked on foot and were healthier than this generation.

(Baba shouts to a devotee who walks with fast steps through the ashram: "You go slowly!") **Everything in life has its own time and therefore requires patience.** If we have prepared a meal on the stove, we should wait for it to cool down before we eat it, otherwise we will burn our mouth. If we undertake a journey, we need to wait until we arrive at our destination. I know what is good for you. The English term "To be patient" means to be patient like a patient. Baba is the doctor.

If you can wait, then God will give you everything! Do not pay attention to whether He comes to the darshan or not, whether He talks to you or not. Baba knows the right time for everything. Baba calls you when you expect it least. **Patience is the most important quality you can foster. He who has patience has an easy life. He is the master of his life.**

Devotee: *Baba, you never lose your patience. We admire this greatly.*

BABA: What you experience here is only a tiny part of my patience. For centuries I have had to wait for my devotees until they finally find their way back to me. **If you are patient with me, then everything in your life will turn into gold.**

PEACE

Devotee: *When in our lives can we reach peace?*

BABA: Peace permeates human life in many ways. Spiritual peace is the light of the divine empire. Concentration is the way to the tower of the peace. **Deep concentration creates an inner peace.** Maintaining this concentration demands spirit and willpower. It continues on its spiritual path until the soul reacts. The soul is meant to develop further and realize God. **The stronger the attraction between God and the soul, the stronger is the basis for peace.** Peace is a two-way street: it comes from divine power and it bestows divine power.

Peace is the source of joy. Peace comes when the truth is discovered. As soon as we can make serious efforts in that direction, we will find the truth and therefore find peace. Efforts made in good faith will be undoubtedly rewarded. But the problems that we encounter should be sufficiently mastered. Then we will be at peace.

I am not talking about physical peace, but the peace of the soul. The peace that lightens the soul touches the lotus feet of God. It is the peace that makes the world a place worth living, full of spiritual brightness. Spiritual peace is superior to any other type of peace.

Devotee: *How can this peace be reached?*

BABA: One's mindset can either lead to peace or dissatisfaction. It is true that in this world, we must struggle for our very existence. We must do our duties, but we must do them peacefully. Our duties are

Sri Balasai Baba

not burdens but responsibilities, tests of skill. Where mental tensions exist, peace will disappear. Our way of thinking, our life planning and our ability to effectively carry out our duties all impact our likelihood of attaining peace.

In human life, peace is precious. Peace does not simply come; we must work for it. In general, most people live their lives in a deplorable way, precisely because they lack this art. A peaceful way of life is nothing other than an art. This art has to be cherished with vision, diligence and understanding.

This fact eludes a lot of people. If one's entire life is only used to get a loaf of bread, if most of our time is spent in search of material livelihood, then we will forget how to live a spiritual life. We will forget about the creation of the inner world of bliss, the world that recites the names of God. Here one has the freedom to choose one's lifestyle. The devotee should never forget the basic right to live peacefully.

In the modern world, natural treasures are frequently destroyed. In so doing, we create a rift between ourselves and the natural world. I am deeply concerned about that. Peace can spring from the environment when it is kept clean and natural. The greater the artificiality, the greater is the imbalance. The starting point of peace lies in the inner world of the consciousness. Nature needs to be protected to guarantee a peaceful inner world.

I will tell you a story. Once upon a time, a family lived a very well-to-do life. They were rich, but their wishes were so numerous that they exhausted their wealth and became poor. They tried hard to return to their former standard of living, but they found themselves unable to do so. The future seemed hopeless.

Finally the family moved away from society, into nature. There they searched for peace and prosperity. They found a little village as a refuge. They blamed their problems on society, laying blame on everybody but themselves for weaknesses that were, first and foremost, their own.

Their tiny village was a truly natural environment. The skyscrapers, air pollution and crime of the big city disappeared from their lives. Nature could have consoled them in their troubled time. But they could not focus on anything but wealth and success. They lacked the characteristics of a peaceful, loving nature. The family began to exploit the natural treasures around them, cutting down trees and seizing all the natural resources that could be used.

Eventually, however, they came to understand that wealth, abundance and power are not the only important things in life. Life is a holy duty. Duty is what makes life worth living.

The family recognized this principle and stopped exploiting nature. They erected cottages made of wood and grass and lived a simple life from then on. The family finally found God through nature. They started to meditate and read the Holy Scriptures. They recited the names of God.

They invited the people of village to sing praises to the Lord with them. They grew corn and provided themselves with livestock. Cows provided milk, with which they prepared the blessed meals that they then offered to God and the people of the village. Thus they could find peace in the light of God.

If somebody becomes aware of his own weaknesses, then he can change them. Perceiving your weaknesses is the first step towards correcting them.

Most people have forgotten these human values. The important parts of their lives are missing. The individual yearns eagerly for material progress, but not for spiritual growth. If a spiritual life is adopted, then the eternal fragrance of peace permeates everything. Peace is the key to progress.

Devotee: *What happens when we pray for peace?*
BABA: Pray - then peace, love and joy will come automatically whenever you connect with me through prayer. **Pray: "Baba, please bestow peace unto every being in the universe."**

Every part of the cosmos is also a part of me. Therefore, pray for yourself, too! Once you are at peace with yourself, then you can ask for peace for others. Everything begins with yourself. The first step is not to make others suffer on an emotional or physical level. Then you can be at peace with yourself.

Peace should be a permanent state, not a temporary phase. People should respect each other's rights. In this way a complete harmony of thinking and acting can be attained. Peace might be partially determined by our circumstances, but it is our mental attitude that dictates our peacefulness or lack thereof.

The role of peace in human life is very important, since without peace life will be empty. The fruits of life can only be harvested if one duly plants the tree of peace. Under the protection of such a tree, we can experience the breath of the wind of unity, the blossoms of friendship, and the fruits of solidarity.

Let peace come to the lives of all beings. Let peace spread its arms to embrace all religions and nations of the world!

Each January, the international world peace conference takes place. The conference is dedicated to world peace and takes place on the site of the Sri Nilayam Ashram in India. Its proceedings enjoy the blessings of Balasai Baba. Important figures from all over the world participate, exchange ideas and commit to action that will help secure peace for the entire universe.

PRAYER

Devotee: *Baba, what happens if we pray to you from the depths of our hearts?*

BABA: My heart starts to shake and a sort of communication commences between you and me. I will then listen to what you want to tell me.

Jesus said, "Whenever you pray, be awake and be present with your full heart." Whatever you seek through your prayer or meditation will be freely given by God. But be aware that although your lips utter one wish, your heart may really desire something else. God does not listen to your words. He only looks at your heart. When you pray to God, you should convey your true wishes and thereby stay mentally awake.

Pray and surrender your wishes to me! Then do not worry about the results. When you put money on a bank account, you can have confidence that the money shall be deposited. It is like that here. Pray! Your job is to pray! My job is to help bring about peace on earth.

God is like electrical power. You might not always be able to see Him, but if you erect a power line, put a bulb into the socket and switch on the circuit breaker, your houses will be illuminated.

A person who has laid his life at my feet does not need to wish for anything. I will always take care of him and give him what he needs. The time you invest in God will yield good fruit.

Devotee: What should my prayer sound like?

BABA: Your prayer should sound like this: "O God, what do I get from this world? Only affliction, suffering and pain. There is no lasting joy. I have lost interest in this mundane existence. O God, how I suffer from separation from you! Please liberate me from the circle of death and birth, as well as the sufferings connected with that circle. My God, let me always be with you, so that I will live in the eternal joy and love that you are. Please, let me be one with you!"

You should pray to the divine form to which you are most attracted. Pray from the depth of your heart. It is a divine gift to God's children that they may select the form they most want to worship. The roads to God are many. All religions show you the way to God; they share that same goal.

Your spiritual exercises should be of high quality. If you are happy while performing them, God will also be happy. Singing, meditating, or repeating God's names are all worthy exercises, if

you perform them with joy. God wants only your heart! If you open your hearts, you will discover true love. Live your lives as innocent children. Be like a white sheet of paper. Intellectually you can grow, but in your heart you need to be like a sweet little child.

Devotee: *Baba, we often recite the following prayer: "Oh Mother, lead me from the untruth to the truth, lead me from the darkness to the light. O Mother, lead me from the mortality to immortality".*

BABA: Do you know the meaning of this prayer? It is a great prayer! All of creation is based on the divine game, in which God is the playwright and you are the actor. At the beginning of creation, God gives you life. Then He gives you free will and you go your own ways.

After some time - and after a lot of lives throughout which you collect your own experiences - you will find out that you are a part of God. You will wish to be united with Him. Here begins the spiritual path. Focus on God; recite his name and thereby forget yourself. You should try to see God everywhere and in every human being. When you have decided to do that, He will guide you!

Prayer can be very powerful. A woman used to sit in her prayer room and chant the same prayer every day. For about twenty days she had been sitting in front of her altar, praying to me and asking me to appear in front of her since she was not able to come to the temple. I heard her prayer and sent her some beams of light, which suddenly shone on the photos of me that she kept in the prayer room.

She was stunned, for it was her first experience of this kind. She looked attentively at the photos. Then my form in the photograph changed into that of God Shiva, whom she loved and venerated. She was very happy.

Last week I had her come to the ashram. I called her to me. Immediately she spoke about her experience to make sure that it was not her imagination. I described to her everything exactly as it happened, in full detail. She was very happy. The prayer that she recited is very powerful. It describes the magnificence of God.

PRESENT

Devotee: *Why don't you tell us about your past or future?*

BABA: Do not worry about the past or the future. A human should live in the present. If you focus on the past unnecessarily, it can be a painful experience. Sorrows overwhelm you. Why should you torture yourself? The past is dead - to ponder about it does not make any sense.

And if you ponder unnecessarily about the future, then you might be overwhelmed by fear of the unknown. The future will come on its own. It does not yet exist for you. So what will you gain if you occupy yourself with it? With such thoughts you will only kill the present by not meditating on God. Today is Saturday. You should not expect Sunday, since it will come automatically. The future is not in your hands and you do not have the right to think about it.

Practice the art of being aware. Life is always now and in the present. If you die one day, your thoughts shall rest with God; He liberates you from the circle of life and death. Forget yourself. If you have a baby, you are busy with it for hours and you completely forget yourself. You do not exist anymore; you seem to be one with the baby. In such moments you forget all needs and fears. This happens when you always think of God and incorporate Him in your thoughts, words and deeds.

An intelligent spiritual seeker thinks neither of the past nor the future. The past has passed; yesterday is over. The future is uncertain and brings us what has been set out for us. Therefore, be utterly present at all times and do your best each moment. Tend to perform your duty peacefully and happily.

Sri Balasai Baba _____

REINCARNATION

Devotee: *And what about the reincarnation of animals?*
BABA: Everything moves in the karmic circle; everything dies and is born, dies and is born - eternally. This applies to animals, as well.

Devotee: *What about clairvoyance – seeing our past lives?*
BABA: How would this benefit you? If somebody tells you that you were a monkey in the last life, how will you benefit? You cannot check to see if they are correct. **Do not waste your time with the past!**

I will tell you a true story to illustrate my point. Here in the federal state of Andrah Pradesh, there was once a kingdom ruled by a powerful king. One day, his palace was attacked by the soldiers of a neighboring kingdom. The king was killed and his wife was burnt to death. She was reborn in Los Angeles, in the United States. One night she fell into a trance. Suddenly she found that she could speak Telegu, the national language of Andrah Pradesh. In Telegu, she lamented: "O what have you done to me? I will take revenge on you."

The family of the young lady was desperate. They asked for advice from a local psychotherapist. Fortunately, the psychotherapist was Indian and he understood the problem immediately. He recommended that she travel to Andrah Pradesh as soon as possible. She did so.

Sri Balasai Baba

When she got out of the train, suddenly she could recall her former life as a queen in Andrah Pradesh. Immediately she wanted to visit the palace where she had lived in former times. But the palace had been made into a monument. She insisted that she again be allowed to dwell in it. She was able to identify people around the monument as important figures from her past life, but of course those people had no idea who she was.

Without a visa, she finally had to come back to the United States. She went back to the therapist. Eventually, he saw no other possibility than to prescribe her medication to make her forget her experience.

What is the moral of this story? **We should not dig into past and forgotten matters. We should try to live in the present. We should try to do some good in this lifetime.**

Devotee: *But Baba, a lot of people are interested in learning about the past. Why shouldn't I then be interested in the history of my soul?*

BABA: There was once a great soul, a saint who asked God about reincarnation. God replied, "I will present you with a task to complete, so that you can better understand. Go on foot to the East. There you will reach a site where you will find a muck heap. In this muck heap you will find a little insect. Ask this insect where it comes from."

He performed obediently. When he found the muck heap, he discovered the insect, but before he was able to ask about its origin, it fell dead. Depressed, the saint returned home, where he prayed to God and related the story to Him. God consoled him and He sent him to the West to find about the origin of a pigeon. He went and found the pigeon, but once he saw the pigeon, it immediately fell dead. Again the saint returned and told God what had happened. This time God sent him to the North to meet a cow. When he stood in front of the cow and looked at it, it died. Completely depressed, the man came back.

Finally he was sent by God to the south to meet a young man. When he saw man, the saint immediately asked him, "How are you? Where do you come from?" Beaming, the young man replied, "O wise man, do you not recognize me? I am the insect, the pigeon and the cow that died when you looked at them. Through your holy blessing, they could die and they could be reborn. I thank you. Now I am finally able to come to earth as a human being. God has looked favorably upon me. I am ecstatic."

What can we learn from that story? First, that reincarnation is a fact. Secondly, animals are, like us, bound to the circle of birth and death. Finally, to be born as a human is a great gift from God.

Devotee: *Baba, I went to a reincarnation therapist and experienced two guided returns. I have seen you as an extraordinary human being and not as an avatar. Is that possible that you have become what you are now through the course of many previous lives?*

BABA: It is not like that. I come and go. God can assume any form and sometimes He seems to be an ordinary human being.

RELIGION

Devotee: What are religions?

BABA: Human beings have locked up God in a picture frame. They have a more or less a concrete idea of what God is, where God is, what God has to do, how He has to behave and how He acts. They give a name to this framed picture, calling it a religion.

Why do you identify yourself with a particular religion? Simply be yourself. When you are born, nothing belongs to you and you do not belong to anybody or anything. The humans in your environment gradually talk you into identifying with your name, your social group and your religion. It is put over you like a costume. However, in reality you belong to yourself alone. You are yourself. Be yourself.

I do not want to say that it is not good to adhere to a religion. All religions aim to serve God; therefore their goals are noble. Each religion is equal. **The essence of all religions is love and humanity**. Each religion seeks only the spiritual betterment of humanity.

Devotee: Would you consider the adherents of all religions to be your devotees?

BABA: Yes, it does not matter whether devotees pray to me in particular. Whomever you worship, be it Jesus Christ, the prophet Mohammed or Balasai Baba, you all respect the same God. The humans pray to whom they are attracted; they do not need to pray exclusively to me. My blessing is for all humans who pray to God.

God is responding

Treat the practitioners of all religions with the same respect, but do not talk about them or compare them to one another. The goal of all religions is the same. They only differ in how they approach that goal. We respect all paths, since they all lead to the same God.

The essence of all religions is love! Whether we are talking about Christianity, Islam, or Hinduism, the main message is always love. If love flows from the depth of our hearts, it extends into infinity. We should decide to give hatred and violence no place in our hearts; instead we must create a paradise of love.

Only God is important. Everything else is unimportant. If you repeat this sentence over and over again, if you make it your holy mantra, your negative tendencies will disappear and you will become divine. Dedicate yourself to the service of God and your fellow human beings. In serving others, we serve God, for God lives in each of you. **But first you must develop humanity. Divinity then comes automatically.**

Devotee: *What makes a good religion?*

BABA: Most of today's religions are out of date. Although most people know that they live in a world of illusion and imagination, they want to stay in that world. Which religion takes you directly to God? Which one gives you God's business card? When people only repeat what the priests say, how can there be character development or true spiritual growth?

You cannot immediately possess the qualities of an angel or of God, but you can act as if you already possess them. If you follow my divine instructions, these qualities will slowly but surely manifest themselves. My religion is always vivid, new and eternal. As long as the human race exists, love and humanity will always be necessary.

Devotee: *Is everything that you teach based on the holy Hindu scriptures?*
BABA: I am beyond all scriptures, but I love them all equally. If you want to write a message down, you need a pad. My message is based on Hinduism. I have my own laws and theorems. Nobody can truly understand what I am. You cannot describe God.

Devotee: *And what do you say about philosophy?*
BABA: Be free! Do not get attached to any of the fixed philosophies. Think freely.

Devotee: *I am going to present you a discourse on mysticism in the East and in the West. If you are beyond scriptures, then can I say nothing about you?*
BABA: In this discourse, you will first talk about western mysticism, then eastern mysticism. But at the end you must emphasize: **What we really need is to practice love for one's fellow human beings. We need to cultivate the capacities for love, understanding, patience, tolerance and all the good characteristics that human beings are capable of.**

We should not speak about religion, caste or race. Everybody is equal. God is everywhere. **It is even better to speak about your own experiences. Then you will reach directly the hearts of your listeners.**

Devotee: *Baba, is Hinduism the mother of all religions?*

BABA: It is like the language of Sanskrit, from which many languages have developed. Ultimately, all religions have the same teachings, but they each have their own customs and practices. Sometimes one particular aspect is emphasized. Sometimes another aspect is stressed. Look, the Muslims write from left to right. They want to be different from others. *(Baba takes a biscuit in his hand and bites off a little piece.)* If you are eating a biscuit, you can put it directly in your mouth or you can put your entire arm around your head before you put the biscuit in your mouth. It is completely up to you. The main point is that you eat the biscuit!

Devotee: Some religious movements were born and still exist today. Other religions do not exist anymore - why is this, Baba?

BABA: All religions that have ever existed still exist today. "God is One!" There are many forms – Jesus, Buddha, Muhammed… Baba will unite all religions. He brings together all races under one umbrella of love and humanity. Baba breaks down the old and useless walls.

God does not want religion. He only wants your hearts. A Christian eats and drinks, a Jew eat and drinks, a Muslim eats and drinks, a Hindu eats and drinks and a Buddhist eats and drinks. **The sun shines and the rain falls with the same intensity on all people, regardless of their caste, creed or religion.** When a Muslim cuts his finger, the blood that flows is no different than the blood of a Jew, a Buddhist, a Hindu, or a Christian. **If we persist in thinking narrowly, everything in life will be narrow. But if we extend our thinking, life will open up to us.**

God is beyond religion. God is above religion, close to religion, under religion and around religion. God is omnipresent.

Sri Balasai Baba

S

SACRIFICE

Devotee: *Do I need to make sacrifices to God?*

BABA: You do not need to sacrifice your life. Sacrifice your cigarettes. People say that they give everything to God, but they cannot even give up such small things as smoking. You can gradually smoke less and less every day. Set your mind to a goal and pursue that goal with firm commitment.

Everybody should devote all his available resources to God. But in reality, we cannot give anything to God that God does not already have. The sacrifices we make are for our own benefit, not God's. We should be aware of this fact when we make sacrifices. God does not need anything. **Whatever you offer to God is multiplied by a factor of ten thousand and comes back to you and your children.**

If you offer God ten euro, you must not think that you have given Him your money. It was God who gave you the money in the first place. What you give Him is only a tiny part of what He has given you. Everything you have comes from God. You can only offer God things that already belong to Him.

Devotee: *Why do people here at the ashram sacrifice coconuts?*

BABA: Those who love God present him with a sacrifice. In the

Occident, people used to kill lambs and give them up for sacrifice. Here we consider the killing of any living animal to be a great sin. Each of God's creations has a heart, even if it is unable to show its feelings. Before you kill an animal, it suffers greatly. It is afraid. Inwardly it weeps bitterly. So here we do not kill. We maintain a vegetarian diet.

In India, the coconut represents a sacrificial offering to God. If you cut open the coconut, the inside is pure white - the color of absolute purity. Your heart must be as pure as the color of the coconut heart, for a pure heart is the only present that can please God. I do not want any lambs.

Even today, many people want to sacrifice parts of their body to me. A lot of Hindus go on a pilgrimage and cut their hair off. But what does God want with all that hair? God is only interested in the purity of your heart.

SATAN

Devotee: *If everything is God, who is Satan?*

BABA: I will tell you a story. Once upon a time, there lived a great saint in the mountains of the Himalaya. He meditated every day and talked to God for hours. He was a teacher of the spiritual path. God loved this devotee very much. God said to his divine counterparts, "Look how this devotee loves me with all his heart. He sacrifices his life for me; he is a great example."

They replied, "We do not really believe that he loves you and trusts

God is responding

you completely. You need to send him some tests." God did not want to test him; God found his faith adequate. But the others did not give him any choice. They insisted on testing the holy man. God sent him leprosy. His beloved devotee recognized immediately that this was a gift from God. He prayed, "O Lord, I love You so much. You gave me this disease so that I could love You more and more."

Gradually, the disease got worse and worse. The man's fingers fell off. Then, one morning worms crept out of his mutilated hand and some of them fell on the floor. When he saw that, he collected them carefully and put them back into the wounds, saying, "You little worms came from my highest Lord. Why should I let you fall down on the ground? Come, I will take you back to the place from which you came."

When the saint's students saw their master so sick, they left him, saying to themselves: "How can he continue to be our master when he suffers from this deadly disease and God does nothing about it?" Only the man's wife stayed faithful to him. When the divine beings saw all this and listened to the man's prayers, they went immediately to his Lord, saying, "You need to make this person healthy again. He is indeed a great devotee of God. His belief in You is as firm as a rock." God healed him immediately. When his wife came and looked at him she could not believe her eyes. She thought that he was a different person and she even wanted to run away. But the divine beings appeared and told her the true story behind the saint's disease.

Just like the saint, you have to pass tests on the way to God. Millions of people might say that they are devoted to God. Out of these million, only a few will have faith and devotion enough to finally merge with God. It is like school: Many reach 10th grade. Only a few of them will get 100 points on their exam. Some of them might get eighty points. Average students will get only 50 points and some of them will even fail. Here it is exactly like that.

You need a strong will and determination to overcome these tests. Somebody might approach you and try to convince that I am not a real master. "He is young!" they will say. "How can he be a master?" They are going to try to drag you to other places and other masters.

SERVICE

Devotee: *What is the difference between selfless service and selfish service?*

BABA: Although they seem to be same, these two kinds of service are actually quite different if analyzed critically. If you receive any sort of benefit *(i.e. a salary)* for your service, it is considered to be a service of a low order.

Selfless service is divine. It is a service that is dedicated to God. An inner happiness permeates us when we perform higher services. **Service to God is the highest kind of service.** It is immeasurable. It is selfless. It is unique. God loves those most who serve the poor and the needy.

I am going to tell you a story: Once upon a time there was a woman living close to a church. She was a street sweeper. Every day she cleaned the area around the church. She was quiet, innocent, selfless and spiritual. Every day this duty-conscious woman did her work as best she could, drawing her strength from God. The churchgoers saw in her a high degree of spiritual beauty.

A rich lady who visited the church on Sunday found that this woman was happier and more content than she was. She asked the street sweeper how this could be, but the street sweeper remained silent. The rich woman grew envious of the street sweeper, always looking at her with a nasty and disapproving glance.

One day the street sweeper accidentally touched the rich lady with her broomstick as she was sweeping. The lady was furious and slapped the street sweeper on the cheek. To her surprise and dismay, the lady lost all feeling in the hand that had slapped the cheek. The hand was paralyzed.

When the street sweeper saw this, she prayed to God and put her dusty hands on the rich woman's paralyzed hand. The hand became healthy again. Surprised by the spiritual power of the street sweeper, the rich woman knelt down and touched the street sweeper's feet in veneration.

Devotee: *Is it better to serve selflessly or to pray?*
BABA: If you can, do both. God has given you a healthy body; use it for good things. **If you are blessed with strength, then you shall employ it for good purposes. If you are intelligent, then you shall use this ability to do good things. If you are wealthy, this too should you use for good. Whatever you possess, you should do good things with it.**

SEXUALITY

Devotee: What do you say about sexuality?

BABA: Too much sexuality is unhealthy. The sorrows and anger brought about by such a lifestyle can shorten your lifespan and facilitate premature ageing.

Devotee: Am I responsible for my own bodily urges?

BABA: Everyone is responsible for his or her own behavior. Greed and dependency are the sources of hatred and envy. It is important to keep your bodily fluids in the body as powerful sustainers of your own life. If sexual energy is unnecessarily wasted, you will age more rapidly and lose your enthusiasm for life. If you want to enjoy life, then you should at least think of God. **You will save 1,500 rebirths if you do this.**

Devotee: How should we live our lives?

BABA: Young people think that they should seek all sensual and sexual desires. The beautiful God Manmata and his wife Rati are responsible for these ideas in the hearts and minds of human beings. They sit together and think only about sexual pleasures. They sneak into the thoughts of humans, triggering sexual desires. They do not let them go until these desires are fulfilled. They exert great power over human beings. **At any moment, if the sweet name of the Lord is not on your mind, they will try to enter into your thoughts.**

God Himself is happiness. God created nature. When father and mother happily unite, the fruit of their happiness is a child. Sexuality is therefore a special, holy and powerful force that should only be used for God's holy purposes. Do not use this power like an animal. Do not abuse the source of your happiness. When precious sperm is wasted, you will lose your own life and body force.

In the West you enjoy a lot of sexual freedom. Independent of a person's age, social status, marital status, or even gender, they do what they please. Are there any limits at all?

In India, these things are not possible. If a man approaches a woman, he must accept the consequences of his actions. Before the wedding there is no sex. The parents make sure that young people finish first their studies; for that they need all their energy. Their thoughts might be already with the other gender, but they need to wait until the parents begin planning the wedding. According to Indian tradition, a man stays with the members of his family, who feed and take care of him so that he will be strong and healthy when his wife comes. Even when the three months of waiting are over and the bride may sleep at her husband's house, the act of love may not occur spontaneously. Even today a lot of couples consult a priest to ascertain the most auspicious time for love, based on the planets and constellation. In India we say that the couple should not meet before twelve o'clock and that during the act of love, nobody else should be present. Observing the act of sex is considered a sin.

The couple dedicates the act to God and is totally concentrated on Him. In order to give birth to smart and healthy children with good foundations for a strong character, most couples stick to these recommendations. Then the child will be able to face life. You in the West do not know anything about that. That is why you do not behave accordingly.

If you want to have sex, then you should marry and give birth to children. Take responsibility for your actions. Do not behave like animals, but like true humans. If you believe that you can live without sex, then you stay single and dedicate your entire life to God. In India a lot of people still respect God; the majority believe in God. In the West these values have - generally speaking - disappeared. This is one reason why there is so much sexual abuse.

Nowadays people are crazy about sex. Do you know why? Because sex is a bit like heaven on earth. If you are deeply absorbed in sex, you will forget everything else around you. You concentrate only on the sexual act. No noise, no thought disturbs you. But your happiness lasts only a few minutes.

The object of your intense concentration should be God alone. In the same manner that you withdraw your senses from the world and direct them towards the sexual act, so should you direct your full attention to God. Transfer your worldly desires into a deep longing for God. If you choose this way, you won't lose anything. You will only receive.

You therefore have a choice. If you dedicate your life to God, He will take care of everything. So be aware. Call the names of God. Bring His form into memory and then He will take care of you. If you completely merge with Him, then He will also absorb your sexual thoughts.

Devotee: What is the difference between we Indians and those in the West?

BABA: People everywhere are the same, but in India they still believe in the reality and the existence of God. And our women generally have only one man. Despite Jesus' teachings, in other parts of the world it is otherwise. A few Indians are polygamous, but even if they prostitute themselves they often pray daily to God. I always teach my devotees that the reasons for all sufferings and crime that prevail in the world are the three W's: Wine, wife and wealth. These three things can make people lose their character and become criminals.

Devotee: *Baba, many people are nowadays afraid of AIDS.*

BABA: AIDS is a dangerous disease that spreads very rapidly. Many babies nowadays are born with AIDS. You have to be careful. Blood and bodily fluids carry the virus.

Many people are not afraid of AIDS, because it is invisible. They think: First let us have pleasure. Later we will see what happens. They take comfort in the fact that the sickness is invisible; nobody will be able to tell if they have it. For this scourge to end, divine order must return. We must pursue pure love, compassion and the development of a sound character.

SIN

Devotee: *How should I pay off my sins?*

BABA: The singing of holy songs and the carrying out of spiritual practices is sufficient to make up for your sins.

Devotee: *As a Christian I was told that I am guilty and that I am sinful before God. Is that true?*

BABA: Here I am telling you that you are not a sinner. If you have feelings of guilt, then you can get rid of them by doing good things. Each religion has its own laws. You should not waste time thinking about them; choose the direct way to God by simply living. Human beings make mistakes. That is human. **God is here to forgive you. Forgiveness is divine.** But we are not allowed to sin deliberately. If we do, that is truly a sin - God does not forgive all sins.

All founders of religions came to earth to tell humans about the good, about love and humanity. They did not come to write about evil and sin. Later on, people generated their own laws to keep their own religious movements alive and to preserve their own religious identities.

SLEEP

Devotee: *How much sleep is necessary?*

BABA: Try not to sleep during the day. Eight hours of sleep each night is sufficient. Only if you do not get enough sleep at night should you make up for lost sleep during the day.

Instead of sleeping at night, try to think of me and meditate. When you are tired, sleep a little bit here in the ashram during the day. All yogis meditate at night. Between the early hours of three and six o'clock, you should contemplate God, pray and meditate. This will bring you great benefit. I recommend this especially for those who do not need to work. For those who need to work eight hours a day, a different schedule might be better. But if you live only for God, prayer is your duty.

SOCIAL PROJECTS

Devotee: *How can we support you?*

BABA: If you want to do something good, you can support the social projects of Sri Balasai Baba. The money I receive will be used wisely. The proceeds are used to perform surgical eye operations for the poor, to maintain our hospitals and to purchase vital medical supplies. All medical services are provided to the needy without charge. There is also the Sri Balasai Baba Residential School, which provides free education to children unable to afford the small tuition fees.

Baba's projects are good opportunities for you to do something good for the world. It is not only good for you, but also good for those who benefit from the projects. Humans are capable of doing good things, if we can find out how to melt their hearts. **Each heart can be melted. We only have to find out how.**

Money needs to circulate constantly, like blood. When blood does not circulate correctly, it comes to a standstill. Standstill means death. Everything that we hide is going to spoil, stink and die. We have to show what we have and to make it available. On earth, everyone should be a little Sai Baba. Money that does not circulate will spoil.

Sri Balasai Baba

Devotee: Why is that man praying?

BABA: He never eats without sitting in prayer for one hour before the altar. First he takes a bath, then an hour of prayer. Then he eats. He does not even touch coffee or water without remembering me. He loves me very much, feels me at his side and thereby he is very happy. He has full confidence in me and thinks about Baba all the time. I love him very much; he is a good man. He has done a lot for society. He is a former politician, but soon I will give him back his position, for he still has great influence. He is healthy and rich and very interested in spiritual growth. He supported the construction of the ashram and he has already invited me to his town to talk to the people there. He has invested a lot of time and money in worthwhile projects. Beside my blessings he does not seek anything.

Devotee: Baba, could you tell us anything about the eye-camp you started? Why was this eye-camp founded and what function does it serve today?

BABA: In India in particular, many people suffer from eye diseases due to malnutrition, extreme sun radiation and extreme poverty. In order to help these people, we built eye camps to provide them with free surgical care. When they get back their eyesight, they will be able to help their families and become fully integrated members of society.

Indian physicians are paid from the people's own pockets, not by insurance companies. A computer tomography costs more than the salary of a government official. Most Indians cannot afford to pay a physician, so we organized a camp to give people treatment for ailments of the eye. The first eye camp was organized in March 1995, in a little village 20 kilometers away from Kurnool. More than hundred thousand people suffer from cataracts, caused by the sun's rays and by the lack of vitamins. It causes near-complete blindness. But in fifteen minutes, surgery can give these people their sight.

Most of the people are so poor that they cannot afford bus travel. This is why Baba's physicians travel to the villages and perform the eye surgeries there. Baba pays for everything: physicians, glasses and nutrition. A school building was transformed into a medical station for the projects. The supervisor, an experienced eye doctor named Dr. Balakrishnamurthy, offered his services without charge.

That was the first eye-camp. More are coming. We are also planning to create free vaccination camps and a new "Super Special Hospital."

Devotee: *What is this "Super Special Hospital" that you want to build? Why do you want to build it?*

BABA: In India, a lot of poor people suffer because they are sick and unable to afford medical treatment. Many die of their ailments. I want to give them good medical care. I want to help them spiritually and materially. I want to build a high-tech hospital built in the style of a temple.

When people come to this hospital, I want them to have the feeling and conscious perception that they enter a temple where they can trust in the help of God. They should be aware that they are in heaven, not in a hospital. Once they arrive at the hospital, they will feel better than before. A feeling of joy will arise in them. We will then provide people with proper medical care. We will use ancient building techniques to build a high-tech hospital as a beautiful temple.

Due to high population density, most people live in simple conditions. That means that only rich people can afford adequate medical treatment in a modern hospital. I want to provide the same quality medical treatment to the poor, so that they can also be healthy.

Devotee: *Is this going to be the first ultramodern hospital in this area?*

BABA: Yes, this is correct. We are going to look at it as a challenge to build a hospital that will serve as a model for other hospitals for the next thousand years. Outside, it will be built according to ancient traditions and plans, but inside there will be modern technology of international caliber. There will be professional treatment and personal patient care.

Devotee: *Baba, what do you mean when you call it a "Super Special" hospital?*

BABA: "Super Special" means that we are going to treat the sick more efficiently and more quickly than ordinary hospitals can. This is crucial in a country like India. There are so many people who have to wait months or even years for medical treatment. So we want to introduce this modern system. We want to employ the latest medical apparatuses. With such highly developed technology, you can help a patient recover quickly. This is a very crucial point for people who have to support their families and do not have time to spend in the hospital. I hope to build the hospital very soon.

Devotee: *Do you believe that you can get adequate personnel to operate the facility? Where will these people come from? Will they be Indians or foreign physicians?*

BABA: Well, we have to address this problem. A lot of people in various countries do work for Baba's foundation. With the help of the devotees and their donations, the premises for the hospital could be purchased. Some devotees also want to finance the construction of the hospital. But we need other help, too. Input is needed from compassionate people who could help us purchase expensive medical apparatuses. God's blessings will flow to those who help us and the joy and the gratitude of the afflicted will be theirs. Everybody, including God, will be happy. **Those who offer their services to this foundation and the divine incarnation will live a successful life, on the material as well as on the spiritual level. They will receive the blessings of God.**

Devotee: *In Europe we have a lot of problems in our hospitals. I want to list some of them and ask you how you intend to avoid similar problems. There are very high maintenance costs. The salaries for personnel and the physicians are very high. Expenses increase rapidly. Sometimes physicians take advantage of the technology instead of respecting the human being holistically. There is also great temptation for physicians to withhold certain treatments, because they are too expensive. Most physicians are also very interested in their salaries. They compete with their colleagues over salaries instead of dedicating themselves to the patients. At a lot of births they perform a Caesarean even if it is not necessary. The food is not very tasty, nor is it very healthy. Those are our problems. How will you avoid them?*

BABA: Such problems won't appear because I am here. I will often be at the hospital myself. When the patients come into this hospital, they will therefore feel more content and happy, because they will know that God is very close. Priority will not be given to surgeries and medical treatments, but to love for one's fellow human. Only if necessary will a surgery be carried out. Modern medical equipment will be used. We will treat the patients with friendliness, admiration and gentleness. We will use our knowledge of cooking to prepare fresh, healthy food for the patients.

In this country there are a great deal of people; therefore there won't be a lack of personnel. The people will work for a meager income but with a full heart. A great number of personnel will guarantee each patient adequate care. Our volunteers and devotees of Baba will joyfully serve their fellow humans. The personnel will receive an adequate salary. There won't be any competition among the physicians, since each of them will be aware that he works for God in the temple-hospital.

Devotee: *Are the physicians going to carry out the art of spiritual healing? Will you teach them this art?*

BABA: Morning and evening, meditation should be performed in the temple. The patients can participate in bhajan singing if they wish. Moreover, we will plan monthly meetings for physicians, nurses, technicians, computer experts, etc. At these meetings the personnel should be taught to meet the patient with love, admiration and friendliness in the temple. The patient should feel like he is in heaven and know that he is in divine hands.

Devotee: *Will the process of healing for patients in the temple-hospital be accelerated by your divine presence?*

BABA: Yes. Patients will find that they need far less recovery time than in conventional hospitals. A patient who needs to undergo a heart surgery is usually stationary for three to six weeks. By divine grace and the power of my blessings, at my hospital the duration of his stay will be halved. He will recover very quickly and will be able go home soon, joyfully and with trust in God.

God is responding

Devotee: We need open hearts, helping hands, wise minds and willing donors to support these projects.

Baba's social projects include the Sri Balasai Residential School, mobile optical care units, the Super Special Hospital and the delivery of fresh drinking water to rural areas. More information is available from the following German, Austrian and Indian charity organizations:

1. Licht-Blick e.V.
Gustav-Ohm-Strasse 68
D- 46236 Bottrop /Germany
Phone: +49-(0)201-690174
www.licht-blick-ev.de

2. Children Are Our Future e.V.
Postfach 34 01 13
D- 80098 Munich /Germany
Phone: + 49-(0)89-35 00 93 25
www.children-are-our-future.com

3. Association
"Helfende Hände"
Schulstraße 25
A- 2763 Neusiedl bei Pernitz
Phone: +41 79 704 95 32
www.sribalasaibaba.at

4. Sri Balasai Baba Central Trust
1-2-593/8, Gagan Mahal Colony,
Domalguda, Hyderabad
500029 Andhra Pradesh / India
Phone: + 91- 40 66 61 36 83
www.balasaicentraltrust.org

SPIRITUALITY

Devotee: Is the spiritual path easy?

BABA: Sometimes you get the impression that the spiritual path lies very close and you that can easily walk on it. It's a fallacy. You become a victim when have confidence in what your eyes see. To your eyes, everything seems to be close. If you approach the object and try to grasp it, you will notice how far the objects lie away.

Devotee: What can we do when we are on the spiritual path?

BABA: On the spiritual path, you should use your reason and set big goals. God gives you what you ask for; it will be a pity if you are satisfied with trivialities. Those among you who cannot make up your minds about what you want in life should decide: I live and die for God. In everything I think, say and do, I will remember Him.

Devotee: Should one be careful on the spiritual path?

BABA: It is important to be on spiritual path in the right company.

Devotee: Can you say something about spiritual experiences?

BABA: **Do not pay attention to the spiritual lives of others! We should not treat the experiences of others as a model for ourselves!** Many people collect many experiences. When spiritual discussions take place, listen only. Do not identify yourself. Do not strive for spiritual experiences. What will happen if you eagerly want to have some experiences but you do not get any? You will sink into depression. Keep your eye always riveted on your fixed goal. Not more! Focus on your goal of union with God.

Devotee: What do I need on the way to God?

BABA: **Spiritual practice. Each word from my mouth is unique. Whatever I say, keep it in your mind and put it into practice.**
In the beginning it will be new for you, but with practice comes mastery. If you study dancing or singing, you need some time before you can become a master. It is exactly like that here. Sometimes an

entire life is not sufficient to realize a single spiritual virtue. So do not wait! Be patient and keep your goal in mind whenever you think, speak and act.

SUFFERING

Devotee: Why did enlightened people like Sri Ramana Maharshi suffer so much physically?

BABA: Spiritually enlightened people do not worry so much about their bodies. The body belongs to the material world. The time that they might spend to enhance their physical well-being is better spent with God. They are at the point when they say to God, "You have given me this body; you may take it back again!" Even if they get cancer or AIDS, it does not matter to them.

Devotee: Is it because of their karma that they suffer that badly?

BABA: No. I said already that these people are enlightened.
Through the course of many lives, they have prepared themselves for physical suffering. They have reached their goal. A lot of them become physically sick, so great is the spiritual energy within them. Only if you are able to see and experience good and evil as the same will you be truly neutral. This is the level of their spiritual achievement.

Devotee: When we suffer, then do you also suffer?

BABA: Of course. I am you and you are me – there is no difference. Therefore it is my wish that you are always happy.

Sri Balasai Baba

Sometimes my heart is a little bit heavy with the sorrows of my devotees, as well as everything that I have seen and experienced on this earth. However, my mother always accepted every situation with a smile. Why should I burden my heart and make it sad with the sorrows of others? Therefore, I am silent when I am presented with difficult problems.

(Baba inhales and exhales deeply) **Look, that is how I do it. Whenever you have sorrows, inhale deeply and discard your burdens as you exhale.** Even when my mother was lying dead in front of me, I did not weep from the depth of my heart, with eyes full of tears. I perceived the pain as a weight on my chest and my face felt a little bit heavy as well. First I swallowed and then I inhaled and exhaled deeply. Thereafter, I smiled as usual to console the families and the devotees who were deeply sad.

SUICIDE

Devotee: *Baba, what happens to the people who commit suicide? Where do they go after their death?*

BABA: They live in the air. Then, they look for a shelter in weak souls or bodies. It is like an empty house being occupied by squatters. Suppose a human would ordinarily have a lifespan of eighty years. If he commits suicide at 40, then he needs to wander around as a bad ghost for 40 years. There is no benefit to suicide.

Devotee: *What kind of karma does a person get when he commits suicide?*

BABA: Committing suicide is not good. Suicide creates bad karma. God has bestowed life to humans in order to be happy, to think of God, to do good things for society, to honor one's country, to support the poor and to render your work a service to the divine. If you lead this kind of life, why then would you commit suicide? You have received your present body because you have done something good in your past life. If you now discard that gift, then you need to start again from the beginning.

T

TEMPLES

Devotee: What is the reason for walking around temples?

BABA: Being in temples generates divine blessings, because one is physically and mentally active. You should inwardly repeat the mantra of Baba when you are there. If you have the power, the patience and the humbleness to walk around the temple of Baba, someday the entire universe will turn around you.

Walking around the temple is more effective than any other spiritual practice, for everything is included in it: body, mind, spirit and soul. You can picture yourself walking around God in your heart. As soon as you bow before a sanctuary or before God, the entire universe will bow before you. Three rounds is the minimum, but it is better to do nine, or as many as you wish.

At the same time you will be closer to Baba. You do not need to tell Baba your wishes. Baba knows what you need and he will fulfill them. Concentrating on Baba will harmonize heart, spirit and body. Good feelings of joy and inner peace will awaken in you and you will be one step closer to achieving the highest goal: eternal happiness.

TIME

Devotee: Is there no meaning of time for you?

BABA: I always choose the right time. Time is in my custody. But you, by contrast, are in the custody of the time. When your time comes, you need to die. I go when I want to.

Every moment in your life is unique; it will never come back. This is especially true of those moments you have spent with me. **Be aware of how precious every moment is. Be aware of why you looked for me. What Baba says is unique; you will never get to hear the same words again. You came to me to ignite the spiritual light that slumbers in each of you. You want to keep it eternally alive. Let this light surround your entire nature. Transfer it to the people around you.**

WISHES

Devotee: Why do we humans always desire change?

BABA: This is human nature. The human heart is always longing for a change; it always searches for something new. This is a big problem. Even when the body is too old for physical love, you long for it. If you are totally entangled in the outer world, how can you then go deep inside yourself and search for God? But if you are in tune with the God that lives within you, then there will be no need for to run after these ephemeral pleasures!

Devotee: Baba, do my wishes influence my mind?

BABA: If you have many wishes, they will tear your mind into a thousand pieces. You must limit yourself to one goal and pursue it. Having too many wishes is like having too many duties. In the end you will find yourself overwhelmed, totally exhausted and unable to accomplish anything. If you decide to pursue a material or spiritual goal, you must remain committed to achieving that goal. If you try to pursue too many material goals at once, not only will you not achieve them, but you will also fail in the spiritual field.

You cannot reach your spiritual goals if you are mired in material pleasures. You will cheat yourself if you think you can have both. It is like standing with your left foot in one boat and your right foot in another boat. If you try to cross the river in this way, both boats will drift apart.

On the one hand, your heart seeks the divine goal of unity with God. On the other hand, you also long for the enjoyment of material pleasures. This back and forth motion generates great pain. Stick to the decisions you have made and pursue your goals relentlessly. By the grace of God and by virtue of your efforts, you will achieve your objectives.

I know that you have heard these words again and again and that you know my teachings. However, I ask you to remember them. It is up to you to put my words into reality.

Devotee: May I touch your feet?
BABA: What do you think when you touch my feet?

Devotee: Om Sri Balasai Ram.
BABA: When you do not have any specific wish then this type of thought is alright. **But you should be aware that when you are with Baba, your wishes will undoubtedly be fulfilled. Therefore, always be awake and do not allow your thoughts to be occupied with things that you may not want. Whatever you think of will become true. Even if you sit in the vicinity of me, the thoughts that occupy your mind during that time will be fulfilled. It is like sitting close to an open fire. The heat of the fire warms all sides. Even those who sit far away will be warmed.**

Talk openly about your wishes. If you keep your wishes in your heart and bury them there, if you deny them expression, then they will take control of you as long as they remain unfulfilled.

Humans are haunted by so many desires and wishes. Mostly they suppress them. You should not suppress a desire, because otherwise you kill the soul. And since God is the soul, you will kill God. Therefore, fulfill your wishes with moderation, so that you are able to focus on God. If you do not, then your wishes will haunt you and your thoughts will always be with your unfulfilled wishes.

Devotee: *Baba, you said that we should not suppress anything. But if we satisfy an unfulfilled wish, then many more of them will follow and there will be no end.*

BABA: **You need to use your intelligence and discrimination to determine whether or not the fulfillment of a wish will ultimately be productive or counterproductive.**

Sri Balasai Baba _____

YOGA

Devotee: *I am a Yoga teacher. Do I need a mantra?*

BABA: You are free; you do not need to repeat a single name. The most important thing is to continue your practices. You are on the right track - continue! You should not be bored. It is also possible to simply think of me without focusing on a name or a form.

Devotee: *As a yoga teacher I ask you: Does our practice show us the path of devotion?*

BABA: This point is very useful for all spiritual practitioners. Yoga postures, meditation, breathing exercises, prayers, songs of praise and holy acts of sacrifices are all equally good. They should help you on the way to God. Their purpose is to help you concentrate on something. When you have achieved full concentration, then your heart will also take part. Spiritual practices are your personal aids on the way to God. **But God Himself wants nothing but your heart and your love.** For Him, the form of your practice is unimportant.

YOUTH

Devotee *(a youngster): What is important for the youth?*

BABA: Young people should not yet walk the spiritual path of liberation. By focusing on liberation, they are in danger of neglecting their worldly duties. They should opt for the path of spiritual devotion to God.

What kind of life do you have when you live only for yourself?
Such a life is a pure waste. Everything that you do for yourself will extinguish when you die. **Only the good things that you have done for your fellow human being - the poor and needy – will come with you into the spiritual world after your death. Sacrifice your bad habits like smoking, drinking and the like. This will preserve your health.**

For instance, if you put aside the money you have been spending on bad habits and instead give it to a good cause, you have not only done something good for yourself, but also for your fellow human beings. Even a single euro it is useful to a poor person. If you live in this way, you will bring honor to your parents and your country.

Being a useful member of human society will benefit yourself and your fellow human beings. Do not be lazy in the name of God! If you want to reach your goals, then you need to work for them. The future of the country depends on the younger generation. Therefore, do not be a shame to your parents and your country. Be useful! Do not sit around and wait for God to do things for you! You have to make efforts. Then divine grace and blessings will come to you. Fortune and

God is responding

God are the same. Fortune always waits to help you, but you have to be ready to receive it. Do not blame God if you live in hell. Your thoughts and actions create hell for yourself.

Our choices early on will determine the later courses of our lives. Just as we save and invest money in order to benefit from it when we are older, so we should invest in a good character at a young age. If you waste your youth, as a result you will probably suffer when you are older. If you are already a little bit older, then do not think that it is too late for you to change your ways. Forget your past. Change your life today! If your life spans 100 years and you are 50 years old, then you still have fifty years before you. Try to live life according to a system.

If you want to build a seven-story house, you need a solid foundation. If you want happiness and health when you are older, you must begin when you are young. If you develop physical, mental and moral strength, you can easily face the challenges that life brings you.

Live for God! Spread His message. Why should you feel ashamed to spread his message? You feel no shame at things you should, but when it comes to spreading God's message, all of a sudden you are ashamed.

Before you can reach God, you need to develop humanity. Learn how to love each other. Help each other. Do not be selfish and proud. Only if you develop good human characteristics you will be able to reach God.

There is a boy who now lives here at the ashram. He is now twenty-one years old. Two years ago I called him to me. He was a problem child, what we call a Street Romeo – a troublemaking youngster living on the streets of a big city. This boy was addicted to drugs and alcohol. While drunk, he vomited wherever he pleased, yelled at his parents, beat his parents and stole money from his brother. He was a very dangerous young man. He became a burden to everybody who had to live with him. He had ruined his life.

With my love I have completely changed him. He became a very soft and loving sort of person, absolutely unable to harm anybody. Today it disgusts him when he smells cigarettes or alcohol. He never drinks or smokes. He spends most of his time here, working with joy and diligence and singing bhajans. He is content with his life. **True happiness can only come from God.** One does not need to take drugs to have high feelings. The happiness that comes from God can be so strong and beautiful that you couldn't describe it with words. If you remember God, you will lose your interest in dangerous drugs, for you will be physically, mentally and morally strong. You will lead a long and happy life.

CONCLUSION

BABA: We could eternally talk about God. This topic is inexhaustible. God does not have a true form. He is and stays indescribable. You may have read many books. You should always quench your thirst for knowledge, but it will only be beneficial if you put ideas into practice.
Good things will not come from thoughts alone. Only if we put our thoughts into action will they benefit anybody. Then something miraculous can happen.
I have told you many secrets and answered many questions. What are you going to do with what I have told you?

Addresses of the Ashrams in India:

Ashram Kurnool
Sri Balasai Nilayam
Kurnool 518001, A.P. India
Phone: + 91- 929 825 996 7
+ 91- 958 149 294 2

Ashram Hyderabad
Sri Balasai Nilayam
Domalguda No. 1-2-593-8
Gaga Mahal Colony
Hyderabad 500029, A.P., India
Phone: see above

E-mail: balasai.info@gmail.com

www.sribalasai.com